The MAIN STREETS *of* OKLAHOMA

OKIE STORIES FROM EVERY COUNTY

KRISTI EATON

Published by The History Press
Charleston, SC 29403
www.historypress.net

Cover and internal images by the author unless otherwise noted.

First published 2014

Manufactured in the United States

ISBN 978.1.62619.649.0

Library of Congress CIP data applied for.

Notice: The information in this book is true and complete to the best of our knowledge. It is offered without guarantee on the part of the author or The History Press. The author and The History Press disclaim all liability in connection with the use of this book.

"There are lots of untold stories right here on Main Street."

—Robert Cormier

Table of Contents

Acknowledgements

Writing a book has been a dream of mine for as long as I can remember. Actually, this isn't my first book if you count the handful of picture books about puppies I created in kindergarten and first grade. But this one includes far more words and took much more research time. Because of that, I owe gratitude to a lot of people.

My family, as much as they may have regretted it later on, instilled my adventurous and observational spirit from a young age. Sitting at the kitchen table reading the three newspapers that arrived on our front porch each day at the age of eight, I could only imagine what sort of world laid out before me. I vowed to see, explore and learn about it as much as I could. This thirst for exploration and new experiences led me hundreds, sometimes thousands, of miles away to the dry desert, a tiny Pacific island, the farmlands of South Dakota and, ultimately, back to Oklahoma, where I investigated communities I had never before even heard of.

Richard spent many weekends driving me all over Oklahoma and researching these foreign areas in our own backyards. I would like to think he enjoyed examining Main Streets as much as I did—he did take several iPhone photos and plastered them across social media, after all—but I know, deep down, he gave up his weekends because of how much he cares for me. He supported me from day one when I told him I wanted to write this book, and for that I am thankful.

The Oklahoma Historical Society provided invaluable information about the history of many of the cities and towns I traveled to, and that research is used throughout this book.

The Main Streets of Oklahoma: Okie Stories from Every County would never have been possible without the many community members who didn't flinch when I walked up to them, called them or emailed them out of the blue and asked them to share their stories about living and working on Main Street. I can't thank them enough.

The History Press and Becky LeJeune seemed intrigued by this idea from the start. I'm deeply appreciative of them taking a chance on me and my affinity for Oklahoma's history and quirkiness.

Introduction

From a very young age, I have had a fascination with Main Street and all that it represents: the small-town feel of a community moving at a slower pace, a deep sense of involvement among local residents who care about one another and a friendliness rarely seen in the hustle and bustle of a large city.

As a child, I grew up in Tulsa, a city of fewer than 400,000 with its own street named Main. But on weekends and holidays, I was whisked away to a different world. This world was only one hundred miles to the northeast in southeast Kansas, but it might as well have been a world away. It was a world where car doors were left unlocked, kids were able to walk to the community pool by themselves and Dairy Queen and the local bowling alley were the places to see and be seen on a Friday night.

It was a place where last names were unnecessary and genuine greetings were an expected part of the day. It was a world shaped around a street that brought the community together. At the end of those trips that lasted two to three days, my family and I would get back in the car and drive south until we returned to our neck of the woods, where SUVs crisscrossed streets, oversized homes were the norm and going shopping meant fighting hordes of people looking for discounts at the big-box stores or the major retailers in the mall. This world had a bit of a faster pace to it and far fewer friendly greetings.

As an adult, I found myself once again mesmerized by Main Street and everything it represents in a small town. It's often—but not always—the center of town. It's where people go to eat, to sleep and to socialize.

In Oklahoma, Main Street is also where people can see hulking horse statues pieced together from leftover metal parts or memorabilia from the movie *Twister* or watch an old-time bank robbery come to life. I knew Oklahoma's Main Streets had a lot to offer in understanding how a community was shaped, so I set out to find the unique events, landmarks and people that call the iconic streets home. I crisscrossed Oklahoma, focusing on one Main Street in each of Oklahoma's seventy-seven counties. Part travelogue and part history book, *The Main Streets of Oklahoma: Okie Stories from Every County* shares the hidden, quirky and forgotten stories along these historic streets.

Adair County

Former Buffington Hotel

Corner of Main Street and Williams Avenue, Westville

It doesn't seem like there would be a lot of need for a hotel in Westville, which is just a few miles from the Arkansas border. The far-eastern Oklahoma town of 1,640 people seems to be one of those places that travelers best experience from the comfort of their cars as they pass through on the way to their final destination.

A century ago, it was a far different landscape: Westville was the county seat of the newly formed Adair County and home to two railroad lines. It was determined that tired and fatigued travelers needed a place to stay overnight on their journeys, and so, the two-story, red brick Buffington Hotel was built in 1910.

The opening date of the hotel, which featured more than twenty guest rooms, may have been its greatest downfall. The year it opened was the same year that the county seat moved fifteen miles to the south to Stilwell.

Westville's growth suffered, and soon the town wasn't in need of a hotel as much anymore. The Buffington Hotel was shuttered by the 1930s, and the building was later used as housing before a local man, Bud Rose, purchased it.

Rose, who is eighty years old, said he initially bought the historic building in hopes of renovating and restoring it back to its original grandeur. That never happened though, and the once-magnificent hotel looks as if it has seen better days.

Still, Rose is content in his home. He lives on the first floor, amidst well-worn furniture pieces and antique items, one of the most notable being

A bull's head greets visitors to the former Buffington Hotel in Westville, Oklahoma.

a framed document commemorating the hotel's listing on the National Register of Historic Places in 1983.

Sitting outside the former hotel on a warm winter day in off-white overalls, Rose was guarded at first but eventually offered to give a tour of the property, showing off the detailed finishings.

"It really looks nice if you get it cleaned up," he said. "I can clean this thing up and get it looking good."

Alfalfa County

Hotel Cherokee

117 West Main Street, Cherokee

Back in the mid-1900s, as salesmen traveled through Oklahoma hawking their wares or men stopped on their way to a hunt, the Hotel Cherokee was the place to be seen.

The Hotel Cherokee was built in 1929 to replace a hotel that burned down two years earlier. Catering to businessmen, hunters and other travelers, the four-story building was more elaborate than any other hotel in the area and larger than originally planned.

After his Orient Hotel burned down, Thomas Thompson decided to create a new hotel more grandiose and extravagant than all the others in town. It would represent the growth and expansion felt in Cherokee as the population boomed. When completed, the Hotel Cherokee featured more rooms, more baths, an extra floor and a more spacious dining room than had originally been conceived. It was the premier hotel in all of Alfalfa County.

Unfortunately, just a few short months after it opened, the effects of the Great Depression hit Alfalfa County, crippling any sense of economic vitality.

Both the town and the Hotel Cherokee were able to weather the Depression for a while, but the Hotel Cherokee closed in 1973. The Alfalfa County Historical Society purchased the property in 1980 and housed the Alfalfa County Museum inside it. About two years ago, however, the museum, which featured a piano once owned by George Armstrong Custer's sister, Anna Custer Reed, shuttered, and the Hotel Cherokee once again closed its doors.

The Hotel Cherokee in Cherokee, Oklahoma, is listed on the National Register of Historic Places.

Marty Myers, who was president of the Alfalfa County Historical Society, said volunteers could no longer work at the museum regularly. The Hotel Cherokee was listed on the National Register of Historic Places in 1998.

Atoka County

Restored Phillips 66 Service Station

Corner of Main and Court Streets, Atoka

Blink and you may miss most of the Main Street that runs for just a few blocks through this southeastern Oklahoma community of 3,100 residents. Atoka, the seat of the county by the same name, has two other heavily trafficked streets littered with motels, churches, fast-food restaurants, local diners and retail stores that one envisions when they picture Main Street. Atoka's Main Street, on the other hand, is home to little more than some overgrown foliage.

The exception sits where the streets of Main and Court intersect. There, a piece of history has come alive for visitors to this community that is in the heart of the Choctaw Nation.

The Atoka Chamber of Commerce, a restored Phillips 66 service station, is seen in this photo.

The red brick building with green awnings is a restored Phillips 66 service station that was originally built in 1932. Three orange and black pumps still stand in the front drive, the Phillips 66 emblems prominent, and the pump prices are stuck at thirty-three cents per gallon.

Today, the building houses the Atoka Chamber of Commerce, which promotes economic development and tourism to the area—and, thanks to the building, historical preservation.

The building is a favorite for picture taking, of course, and many people stop inside and reminisce about the time when their relatives worked there, said Jewell Darst, the chamber's secretary. Others stop by with a simple request to fill 'er up—joking, of course—at least in most cases.

Beaver County

Lane Cabin Marker

Old Main Street and Avenue C, Beaver

Jim Lane may have been ahead of his time. Long before the big-box retail stores like Walmart offered one-stop shopping for lettuce, pantyhose, video games and a bedsheet all under one roof, there was the Lane Cabin. Built in the 1880s along the Jones and Plummer Cattle Trail in the area known as No Man's Land—later the Oklahoma Panhandle—the cabin doubled as a trading post offering cattlemen all the supplies they could possibly need: everything from beans to coffee to whiskey.

The ambitious Lane had come to the area with his family from Dodge City, Kansas, and quickly became the go-to source for new settlers looking for much-needed supplies during their time on the sparse frontier. But as the Panhandle population boomed, competition grew among traders when new sod houses started popping up with the establishment of Beaver City, later renamed simply Beaver.

Over the years, as all the other sod houses disappeared, Lane's Cabin on Old Main Street remained, and it became the oldest man-made structure in the town of Beaver and the entire Panhandle. It was placed on the National Register of Historic Places in 1974.

After Old Main Street, which runs east–west, was flooded, the north–south Douglas Avenue became the main thoroughfare through town. It's a unique—albeit smelly—event that takes place each year just off that street that has put Beaver, population 1,500, on the map. The World Championship Cow Chip Throwing Contest may be one of the stinkiest events in Oklahoma. It could also one of the strictest: Official rules dictate that chips must be at least six inches in diameter. Any alterations can mean a twenty-five-foot penalty, and any record cow-chip throws must meet international arena layout and measurement qualifications to count.

Still, the chance to be named the best cow-dung thrower must have a certain foul appeal because crowds have been turning out in Beaver for years to witness the stinky competition.

Beckham County

The *Sayre Record and Beckham County Democrat*

112 East Main Street, Sayre

The *Sayre Record and Beckham County Democrat* represents the merging of the old with the new. The old being the *Erick Beckham County Democrat* and the *Sayre Record* its young new competitor.

In 1987, Brad and Dayva Spitzer started the *Sayre Record* as a way to document and record what was going on in their community of about 4,375 people in far-western Oklahoma.

Dayva Spitzer has been involved in the newspaper business since she was a child with her own newspaper delivery route. Later, as an adult in the 1980s, she became editor and general manager of the *Sayre Journal*.

The Spitzers bought the *Erick Beckham County Democrat*, a weekly publication in nearby Erick, in 1997 and merged it with the *Sayre Record*. With a circulation of about 2,500, the new newspaper caters to a broader area of readers, including those in Sayre, Erick and Sweetwater as well as more rural parts of Beckham County. "People want local news, and we do our best to keep things local," Dayva Spitzer said. "We love writing feature articles about our good people in Beckham County."

Spitzer said her favorite part of her job is working closely with the people she loves. Her least favorite part of putting out a community newspaper? Making errors in a story. "Mistakes are a fact of life," she said. "It's the response to error that counts. I do my best to apologize when I make mistakes."

As an editor covering a local community, Spitzer believes she should be heavily involved in that community. That's one reason she is the president

The Beckham County Courthouse in Sayre, Oklahoma, was built in 1911.

A sign outside the Beckham County Courthouse in Sayre, Oklahoma.

The *Sayre Record and Beckham County Democrat* is located along Main Street in Sayre, Oklahoma.

of the Sayre Chamber of Commerce, a role that includes planning local functions like a visit by a circus and an upcoming festival.

Weekly newspapers like the *Sayre Record and Beckham County Democrat* are vitally important to communities, Spitzer believes.

Communities, she said, can't survive without three things: churches, good schools and a great newspaper. In Sayre, that integral community piece is located right along Main Street. Though originally located on Fourth Street, the operation quickly outgrew the facilities, so the couple purchased a building and moved the operations to the 112 Main Street address.

"Main Street is the hub that holds all cities together," Spitzer said.

Sayre's Main Street includes a bowling alley, city hall, coffee shop and, at the very end, the Beckham County Courthouse. Built in 1911 at a cost of $69,000, the building features both Neoclassical and Second Renaissance Revival styles and has one of the few courthouse domes in the state. It may look familiar to movie buffs: it made a very brief appearance in the 1940 film *The Grapes of Wrath*.

Blaine County

Watonga Cheese and Wine Festival

Main Street, Watonga

Imagine a festival dedicated to the deliciousness of cheese and wine coupled with family tradition, art and fun. That's just what Watonga offers residents and visitors to its city of five thousand people at the beginning of October each year.

The Watonga Chamber of Commerce held the first-ever Watonga Cheese Festival in 1976, spawned from the 1940 opening of the Watonga Cheese Factory, one of the state's first cheese manufacturers. The festival was initially conceived as a cooking competition in which each entrant was required to make confections using some sort of cheese. The idea was to promote the use of local products, according to Mary Larson with the Watonga Chamber of Commerce.

Over the years, the festival has expanded to include a quilt show, a fine art show, a car show and a parade. A bike race and road race help those who may have over indulged in cheddar curds, bacon cheddar or onion cheddar burn off excess calories.

"We often say that Watonga's legacy is cheese," Larson said. People come from all over to tour the factory and learn about Watonga and its cheese history. Still others buy gifts online from the factory and ship them to friends and relatives in far-flung locales.

In the late 1990s, as the wine industry started to blossom in Oklahoma, vendors with crisp white and light-bodied red wines were added to the festival mix. When the wine industry continued to cultivate in Oklahoma, the festival committee decided the Watonga Cheese Festival would also become a showcase for locally grown wines.

These two photos show early Watonga Cheese Festivals. *Courtesy of the Watonga Cheese Festival.*

With appetizing cheeses and savory wines on the menu, the Watonga Cheese Festival seemed to be headed for long-lasting prestige. But all that changed in 2007. That was the year that eighty-mile-per-hour winds and voluminous rain whipped Watonga, damaging several buildings, including the cheese factory. Casey and Brandi Cowan, who purchased the company in 2002 and learned the signature recipe and processes, opted to reopen the facility in Texas. Though the cheese is still sold throughout Oklahoma, including in Watonga, the city that held a festival every year dedicated to its product felt a bit lost once its signature destination closed shop.

"This created a bit of an identity crisis for Watonga and, more specifically, the festival," Larson said. It led community leaders to ask, "Was the festival's focus Watonga Cheese or Watonga?"

Ultimately, Larson said, leaders decided that after decades of holding the delectable event in Watonga, the focus was meant to be on the community.

"While cheese is still a huge part of the festival, it has diversified to include so much more, the most important part of which is tradition."

Bryan County

Horse Sculptures

Located in front of Landmark Bank at 900 West Main Street, Durant

I could go out and make horses out of two-by-fours or go buy sheets of aluminum and make horses, but it's the emotion that is emitted from these pieces.
—Doug Owen

Though he never owned a horse while growing up in South Dakota, where horses seem to be as plentiful as people, Doug Owen developed an appreciation early on for the magnificent animal. Horses, the longtime artist said, were the lifeblood of farm life just a few generations ago, only recently replaced by combines, tractors, automobiles and other machinery.

For the past fifteen years, sixty-three-year-old Owen has been using pieces of those machines—bumpers, fenders, even license plates—to create hundreds of sculptures resembling horses. The pieces can range from twenty-five inches to twelve feet tall and hundreds of pounds.

A handful of them stand outside the Landmark Bank along Durant's Main Street, part of a vision that the bank's owner, Mark Landrum, had years ago to bring the spirit of the West to his various banks located across the South and Midwest United States.

From afar, the artwork resembles the large animal, but upon closer inspection, the various pieces of scrap metal stand out. Owen, who is joined by his two adult sons in creating the works, has perfected the creative process over the years. He starts by sketching out an idea and then heads to the studio, where he selects from his vast collection of pipe and metal pieces. Drawing on

Made out of metal pieces, these horse sculptures can be found along Durant's Main Street.

the scrap metal pieces' natural colors and shapes, Owen welds the junk together to form the frame and horse's body.

"What we're trying to do is leave the imagination open in our pieces," he said. "You can tell, obviously, they are horses, but we're trying to be creative enough and use enough varying pieces where there is still a lot of room for imagination, and that seems to be what has helped grow the business. People like that."

Originally sold as outdoor works of art, in recent years Owen and his sons have been marketing the pieces more for fine-art collections to be displayed inside, where Owen believes his creations can be best cared for because they won't sustain the wear and tear of weather extremes.

"You know, you wouldn't go out and buy a new Porsche or a new Mercedes and set it out in a field and never look at it again and expect it to hold up, so that's kind of the idea behind the pieces when we make them," he said. "We don't want them just put out in a field or near a road. We want them taken care of and appreciated as fine art."

And they have been appreciated. Owen's urban horses have been on display across the country, including galleries in San Francisco and New York City, and have been sold to collectors from coast to coast in the United States and in more than thirty-five countries.

The artist's success, though, is not based on luck but on good fortune, Owen said. There are countless artists striving for the same success—and many who are better, he said—and that's why keeping his nose to the grindstone is important.

"You have to keep working to get better and you have to be humble enough to accept criticism and try to put it to practice when somebody tells you, you need to do this or do that," Owen said. "And I think that is part of our success."

Caddo County

Johnny Bench Baseball Museum

202 West Main Street, Binger

Though he may have been born sixty miles away in Oklahoma City, make no mistake that Johnny Bench is Binger's claim to fame. Bench, a Hall of Fame catcher who played seventeen seasons for the Cincinnati Reds from 1967 to 1983, grew up in Binger and is known around town as the local boy who made it big.

"The greatest catcher of all time and hometown boy. He made quite a career for himself and had a big impact on the community and Oklahoma itself," said Gary King, a local insurance agent in Binger whose office houses the Johnny Bench Baseball Museum on Main Street.

Located next door to Binger City Hall, the museum features personal photographs of Bench, memorabilia, some of the bats he used in All-Star Games and several of his Gold Glove awards, given each year to the Major League Baseball player who exhibits excellent skill in his respective position, among other items.

Plans for the Johnny Bench Baseball Museum were announced in 2008, and after gathering personal items from locals who knew Bench, the museum was initially located in city hall. But when it outgrew that area, King said the free museum could be housed in his more spacious office next door. Now, King can see as many as a few dozen people each week stop in to admire the collection of Bench items. Summer is usually the busiest time—that's when entire youth baseball teams will stop by Main Street on their way to and from tournaments in the area and learn about the Hall of Fame catcher.

A cutout of Johnny Bench is seen at the entrance of the Johnny Bench Baseball Museum along Main Street in Binger, Oklahoma.

Opposite: Baseball memorabilia sits in the Johnny Bench Baseball Museum.

Of course, for many of the young players, Johnny Bench isn't a household name. He stopped playing before many were even born. Doesn't matter, though, since he's someone who made it big while hailing from a small town. "Those little ones, they have no idea who Johnny Bench is, but the coaches grew up with him so they're wanting to get that tradition instilled—this is what you can do if you apply yourself," King said.

Bench not only excelled on the field but in the classroom as well—he was at the top of his twenty-one-student class in 1965. He still stops by the town of fewer than seven hundred people and has coffee with the locals, King said.

Though the group who initially proposed the museum thought it would create some much-needed economic development opportunities for Binger, the museum does not charge an admission fee, something King believes is necessary to keep the visitors coming by.

"Johnny's heyday was a long time ago, and a lot of the people that remember Johnny are up in their retirements years, so you don't have very many young people coming in," King said. "And the younger people aren't as interested in sports as they used to be. They'd rather play with their phones than play with a baseball bat or basketball or a football."

A sign for the Johnny Bench Baseball Museum hangs on city hall.

A recent vote by the townspeople may move the Johnny Bench Baseball Museum to a new location, on the second floor of a proposed high school baseball stadium. The hope is that the museum will reignite interest in Binger, a community that, like many others in western Oklahoma, has suffered economically over the years as residents move out and businesses close up.

"All the small towns in western Oklahoma have been dying out," King said, noting that stores along main streets are usually boarded up and vacant. "It's sad in that respect, but you have to go where the jobs are...the small towns are dying out."

Canadian County

Yukon's Best Flour Mill

Main Street and South Third Street, Yukon

For decades, the mill that stands along Main Street in Yukon was considered the beacon of the community. The more than one-hundred-year-old structure was owned by two immigrants from Czechoslovakia, John and Frank Kroutil, and their brother-in-law who turned a small-town mill into a worldwide endeavor.

The mill was at one time the community's largest employer, and its impact is still seen at the local school district, whose mascot is the Millers named for the millworkers.

But in recent years, the mill suffered wear and tear, most notably through the burned-out light bulbs on the hulking sign atop the mill that once lit up the night sky. Of the numerous bulbs on the fifty-five-foot-tall sign, only a handful were still working.

That's where Pam Shelton came in. Though not originally from Yukon, Shelton had taught in the local school district for decades and saw how important the mill was to the community's identity. She decided to put a stop to the mill's slow fading and deterioration.

In 2012, Shelton and others created the nonprofit group Friends of Yukon's Best with the goal of raising enough money to get the massive sign back to its original grandeur and repainting the mill.

The first step to returning the sign to its original brightness? Turning off the few remaining lights. The people of Yukon looked at it as a celebratory event, the first step to getting the icon relit. A celebration, called the Blackout

Block Party, was held in June 2012 featuring the band Asleep at the Wheel, known for the song "Get Your Kicks on Route 66."

In June 2013—one year after the sign went dark—Friends of Yukon's Best planned another celebration along Main Street. What was expected to take several years to accomplish was completed: the sign was going to shine brighter than ever with new LED bulbs.

"It was amazing," Shelton recalled of the measures the city's residents took to save and restore the sign so quickly. "Kids saved their pennies."

The group raised the money through a variety of creative fundraising efforts, including selling mill merchandise, Christmas ornaments and old bulbs in mason jars at the Main Street Marketplace, a shop selling locally made products.

"People care about it because we are the Yukon Miller men. That is just our history," Shelton said.

Carter County

Black Theater of Ardmore

536 East Main Street, Ardmore

Deep in the heart of the Chickasaw Nation sits one of the oldest all-black commercial structures in the entire state of Oklahoma. The Black Theater of Ardmore was one of several commercial ventures that catered to the growing black population in the community in the early 1900s.

Though only opened for a little more than two decades, the theater, listed on the National Register of Historic Places, offered black residents of the area a place to experience the same sorts of recreational opportunities and community gathering as white residents during a time of segregation.

Ardmore's black population grew in the 1910s and 1920s as black residents of rural areas migrated to the area seeking employment. Several decades before, when the Chickasaw Indians were forced to move from their homelands in the southeastern United States to Oklahoma, so, too, were the tribe's slaves who worked on tribal members' farms and ranches.

When slavery was abolished, the blacks were freed and allocated land among the Native American tribal members. Over the next few decades, a thriving black population developed business and community ventures in Ardmore, including the Black Theater, which opened in 1922 on Ardmore's Main Street.

The theater was housed in a two-story, red brick building near other businesses owned and operated by black residents, including a barbershop and grocery store, and near the black residential community.

The theater closed around 1944 as the area's black population started to migrate elsewhere, mainly to larger urban areas, and an all-black church purchased the building. Since the early 1980s, the Greater Love Victory Temple Church has occupied the building, holding services two times per week in the historic structure.

Pastor Lee White said the outside of the building remains unchanged, but new doors and windows were installed in recent years.

Cherokee County

Birds Thrift Store

212 East Main Street, Hulbert

Row upon row of books fill one of three buildings that make up the Birds thrift store. Debra Sparks had at one point counted more than ten thousand page-turners in the store along Main Street she runs with her mother, Betty, but she has since lost count.

Receiving, sorting and organizing the voluminous collection of books is Debra's favorite part of operating the store that carries everything from cooking whisks to shoes and electrical cords.

With three buildings chock-full of items either donated or picked up at yard or garage sales, Birds has everything that someone could possibly need—secondhand, at least.

Known as "the Macy's of Hulbert"—so says Betty Sparks laughingly—Birds fills a much-needed void in this town of slightly fewer than six hundred residents.

"It helps people who need, who can't afford to go to all the big stores, who just don't have the money to spend," said Debra, forty-six, a former cashier at Walmart. "I mean, if you're like me, you don't mind wearing used clothes."

Growing up, Betty bought Debra's clothes secondhand and later opened up the store whose name comes from the first initial of the two women and two other family members—Ila and Rebecca—and their last name, Sparks. The women at one time also ran a diner at the store. As Betty, seventy-four, has gotten older, Debra has taken over most of the duties, though her mom still enjoys the hunt for a priceless treasure.

"I've found everything from a bottle full of marijuana seeds to Rolex watches," Betty said when asked about her most unusual finds. One time, she said, a regular customer inquired about a set of jacks and implored her to save the set whenever she came across one. "I said, 'I've got three sets of them,'" Betty said. "She couldn't believe we had those."

The two women say they sell more used clothes than any other item, and Betty has an idea about why: "They're already broken in!" she said.

Choctaw County

Main Street, Hugo

Known as Circus City, USA, Hugo is unlike any other city in Oklahoma. For more than seventy years, this southeastern Oklahoma community has acted as the winter home for the clowns, contortionists and animal handlers who captivate audiences in the spring and summer at their circus performances.

Since 1942, as many as five circuses at a time have called Hugo—population 5,310—home during the cold-weather months. Today, three circuses reside in Hugo during the off-season: the Carson and Barnes Circus, the Kelly Miller Circus and the Culpepper and Merriweather Circus.

Hugo's deep ties to the circus are on display at the Mount Olivet Cemetery, where several well-known circus performers and rodeo champions have been laid to rest.

Known as "Showmen's Rest," the area of the cemetery designated for circus performers has several pillars adorned with elephants and unique gravestones. The cemetery has become a tourist attraction in its own right as visitors come to see the final resting spots for the tightrope walkers, tiger tamers and trapeze artists who lived their lives to dazzle crowds.

Cimarron County

Bombing Replica and Plaque

Main Street Square, Boise City

Cimarron County is known more for its uniqueness than anything else. Positioned in the far-western edge of the Oklahoma Panhandle, it's the only county in the country to touch four states besides its own. (Texas, New Mexico, Kansas and Colorado being the states.) It also encompasses Oklahoma's highest point (atop Black Mesa) and the only community in the state to observe Mountain Time, not Central Time (Kenton).

Aside from the menagerie of facts about what it does contain, Cimarron County is striking for what it doesn't have: people and infrastructure. As the least populated county in Oklahoma, Cimarron has just a few communities, and the county seat of Boise City (rhymes with voice) has just 1,250 residents. There are no stoplights in all of Cimarron County—only a roundabout near the courthouse—and empty, abandoned buildings dot the rural landscape.

That description may make it a little easier to understand—though no less baffling—how American military men could mistake the area for a practice field and drop six bombs on the town and the residents fast asleep in their beds.

On July 5, 1943, a B-17 bomb crew saw the four lights shining from the Cimarron County Courthouse Square and thought they were over their intended target at a practice field in Texas. The bombs were dropped, six in all, one after the other. They narrowly missed sleeping families, a fuel truck and the courthouse.

As the bombs started falling, the operator of the local power plant hopped out of bed and rushed to turn off the lights in the courthouse square.

A plaque and replica of a bomb in courthouse square on Main Street in Boise City, Oklahoma, commemorates the day six bombs were dropped on the small Panhandle town.

With the lights extinguished, the town's thirty minutes of close calls came to an end. The next day, authorities arrived in Boise City to figure out how the diminutive city became a mistaken target. Had the airmen had a little too much fun the night before and one too many alcoholic beverages, ruining their aim? Had they been trying—in a twisted sort of way—to show off for their girlfriends living in Boise City?

Turns out neither of those theories was correct. Investigators said it was simply an error made by an inexperienced navigator covering for a sick colleague.

A replica bomb crater and plaque were dedicated on the fiftieth anniversary of the event at the courthouse square on Main Street. Placed by the Boise City Chamber of Commerce and the Cimarron County Historical Society, the plaque shows a picture of a fighter plane dropping bombs on the courthouse. Above the courthouse, it says, "Boise City Bombed July 5, 1943." Below the dropping bombs, it reads, "Still Booming July 5, 1993."

Cleveland County

Timberlake Rose Rock Museum

419 South Main Street, Noble

Though its nickname (Sooner State) and its blue flag with an American Indian shield may be the better-known symbols of Oklahoma, the state's official rock isn't too rough on the eyes.

The barite rosette, commonly called the rose rock, has been Oklahoma's official state rock since 1968. Joe and Nancy Stine have been running a museum dedicated to the rose-hued rocks since 1971, first in a studio in the back of their home in Norman and, since 1986, in a white house with black shutters along Noble's Main Street.

Noble is the Rose Rock Capital of the World, and where else would the Timberlake Rose Rock Museum be located than in the city that holds a yearly festival dedicated to the crystals formed millions of years ago?

Though Nancy, seventy-nine, and Joe, eighty-four, no longer take part in the festival, you can find the two hard at work at the museum, which sells rose rocks in a variety of sizes along with other Oklahoma memorabilia and trinkets featuring the state bird or the state's red dirt.

"I sell more of those than shot glasses," Nancy Stine said of the dirt jars, a hint of surprise in her voice.

Visitors come from all over the world to see the museum, and according to the guestbook, recent visitors have come from as far away as New York City, Tokyo and Billings, Montana, and as close as Yukon, about forty-five miles away. Some of the pieces for sale at the museum combine the rose rock with Native America. One piece uses tiny rose rocks to document the Trail of Tears, the journey five tribes were forced to make in the 1800s to relocate

Joe Stine works with rose rocks at the Timberlake Rose Rock Museum in Noble, Oklahoma.

Rose rocks at the Timberlake Rose Rock Museum.

The exterior of the Timberlake Rose Rock Museum.

to Indian Territory and present-day Oklahoma from their homeland in the southeastern United States.

The rocks can be found as a single rock about the size of a dime to a large cluster weighing as much as one thousand pounds. Found in central Oklahoma as well as places as far away as Egypt and Saudi Arabia, the rocks were formed when a large amount of barium sulfate built up, creating flat, circular crystal plates that resemble rose petals. The reddish color came from the iron oxide in the sand. Joe, a former geologist, and Nancy used to travel every weekend to dig up rose rocks, but the expeditions are less frequent now. "We used to spend an awful lot of time at it. Every weekend we'd come back covered in mud. Oh my goodness. It was really difficult," Nancy said.

Coal County

Winston Rice

Restoring Clarita and Its Main Street

Winston Rice is on a one-man mission to rebuild his beloved hometown of Clarita, located in southeast Oklahoma. Rice grew up in the coal-mining town before joining the army and heading to far-flung locales including Panama and Alaska. After retiring from the army in the early 1980s, he returned to Clarita in 1987 only to find that the community he had loved for so long had become, in his words, "a dump."

"I was pretty shocked to see that my whole town was gone, pretty much, so I started buying up what I could and restoring them," he said nonchalantly.

By buying the town up, he means he bought and restored a one-hundred-year-old church and a historic cabin that once belonged to a man who had been a scout for General George Armstrong Custer and built a replica of a 1905 blacksmith shop

Main Street, in fact, is largely owned by Rice. It's home to a post office and a rebuilt Schmelzer's building. Originally a blacksmith shop and garage dating back to the early 1900s, Rice purchased the property in 2006 and built a replica of the building. Today, it houses an event hall, and Rice plans to set up a barbecue and smokehouse restaurant inside.

Just across the street sits the compact wooden cabin owned by General "Mule" Wavern, a scout for Custer. But what has gotten the most notice in town may be the restoration of the Clarita Church of Christ. The simple, white wood-sided church has been transformed by Rice into a community building with a new roof. Its fading exterior white paint has been replaced with a deep red, and new bathrooms and efficiency apartments have been added to the layout.

A replica of a building called Schmelzer's that was originally built in the early 1900s on Clarita's Main Street is seen in this photo.

A new bell tower was also added to the roof. "The day I put that bell tower atop that church, everybody went 'wow,'" Rice said of the building that will be used for community events, workshops, weddings, town meetings and other events.

Convincing the handful of people still residing in town that their community can be rebuilt and revitalized hasn't been an easy sell for Rice, but the sixty-seven-year-old, who also owns a tour company in Panama and has taken part in excursions with animal expert Jack Hanna, continues to bring new life to the tiny town and its Main Street. It's on display for thousands of visitors every September when an Amish auction is held just outside of town. Clarita and the surrounding area are home to several Amish residents, and the festival draws visitors to the area to purchase farm equipment, livestock, antiques and colorful, handmade Amish quilts.

Comanche County

T-Mart Express

600 East Main Street, Geronimo

The T-Mart Express is the only gas station in this quickly growing community of about 1,200, located about ten miles south of Lawton. Another gas station, just down the road on Main Street, sits empty and boarded up. Young children ride their bikes through the closed gas station's parking lot, just across from city hall and the police department. It's ironic since new developments seem to be popping up all over Geronimo.

"It's expanding rapidly," said T-Mart cashier Brandon Satcer of the town. Satcer has worked at T-Mart for seven years but lives in nearby Walters.

The customers who venture in to T-Mart each day can run the gamut: a middle-aged man in a hurry to get to his job in Lawton may stop in for a can of Diet Dr. Pepper, or a ten-year-old boy could waste away his afternoon after school looking to spend the little change he found on the side of the road. The difference in the customers is seen in the cars they drive, the items they purchase and how they carry themselves. Money also plays a factor in what life is like for many in the community, Satcer said.

"It depends on how much money you make," he said in describing life in the small town. "A lot of people who work in Lawton, like business owners and whatnot, individuals who own rental properties, that kind of thing, they tend to live pretty quietly where they are. But some of the individuals around here who don't work in Lawton or anything like that, they draw government checks, and those individuals tend to have very erratic lifestyles."

Satcer sees anywhere from twenty to thirty people on a normal day to as many as two hundred during a celebratory weekend.

T-Mart Express in Geronimo, Oklahoma.

A sign along Main Street in Geronimo, Oklahoma.

In addition to the gas station, city hall, a church and a police station, Main Street is also home to many residents living in single-story homes.

The town of Geronimo in southwestern Oklahoma is named for the well-known Apache Indian leader who became a prisoner of war. Geronimo is buried along with family members at Fort Sill Army Base, about twenty miles from his namesake Oklahoma town.

Cotton County

Former B&O Cash Store

Corner of Main Street and Commercial Avenue, Temple

Metal bars cover the Main Street entrance to the old B&O Cash Store in Temple. The only sign that the large building that takes up an entire block was once the "largest country store in the world" is from a fading mural painted on one side.

The mural depicts Temple in its heyday decades ago: women wearing Victorian-style dresses and men wearing suspenders and cowboy hats hustle and bustle around the B&O Cash Store. Horses and buggies and old-time automobiles transport residents to their desired destinations in town.

It's a far cry from today's deserted downtown business district.

"Back in the 1950s and 1960s, it was high times here," said Virginia Dupler, a lifelong Temple resident and volunteer at the local history museum.

Local brothers Bob and Otho Mooney opened the two-hundred-square-foot B&O Cash Store in 1906 with just $1,300. The one-stop shop carried everything anyone could possibly need: it's where residents near and far could buy produce, hardware, equipment for their farms, furniture and clothing. Less than two decades later, B&O had expanded considerably and was grossing $1.5 million each year.

In 1930, the brothers sold their store to Sears, Roebuck and Company, and it continued to serve residents until its closure in 1954. An auto parts store, a grocery store and a factory have all resided in the building, though it now sits empty.

"Like any small town, when you have Walmarts and all that, the town just sorts of dwindles," Dupler said.

Today, the main establishment in the town of one thousand is the Rockin H Land and Cattle Company, a restaurant known for its hearty meals of juicy steaks, fluffy rolls and large baked potatoes. Be prepared to wash it down with water or a glass of beer, though. Liquor by the drink is still outlawed in Cotton County, one of fewer than thirty counties in Oklahoma still clinging to Prohibition-era regulations.

Craig County

Main Street, Bluejacket

Look around in this town of 330 people in Craig County, and you may run into a Bluejacket. It was originally named for Reverend Charles Bluejacket, chief of the Shawnee tribe who moved to Indian Country in the late 1800s from Kansas. A grandson of Chief Bluejacket, Charles Bluejacket was a minister and became the postmaster of Bluejacket's post office.

Today, the town of Bluejacket's post office sits along Main Street, a few short steps from the city hall and the home of the town's current mayor, who also carries the name Bluejacket. Across from the post office is the site where the town's only restaurant and convenience store—hence its name the Store—used to sit before it burned down in 2012. It was owned by—you guessed it—Bluejackets. Chuck and Jamie Bluejacket North owned the store that acted as the gathering spot in the community. Now it's just a piece of concrete slab with newspaper racks near it.

"It's devastating," said longtime Bluejacket resident Bill McHone, who now works part time at the post office across the street. "I mean, that was kind of the hub of the community, and it's no longer. There are people I haven't talked to since it burned down."

There are hopes that some residents will build a new store, McHone said, "but the town is pretty much dying, kid. It's just empty lots everywhere."

To illustrate his point, McHone, sixty-four, stood up from his chair in the post office and pulled out a dated map that showed the plotted areas of town, pointing over and over to the buildings that were hotels, houses and

A building sits abandoned along Main Street in Bluejacket, Oklahoma.

banks—it's believed that Bluejacket once boasted more banks than Tulsa—that are no more.

People started abandoning the town in the 1930s when two tornadoes struck the area, McHone said. One farmer was killed along with several livestock, and several barns were destroyed when a tornado tore through the town on May 4, 1938. A little more than a year later, on August 24, 1939, another tornado sliced through the Bluejacket area, killing two young men and injuring dozens of others. The tornado and large hailstones decimated three businesses and left several other buildings with damage. All told, property damage from the storm approached $500,000.

With an all-time-high population of more than 500 people in 1910, the community lost about 150 residents by 1940, and by 1970, the population was about half of what it had been at its peak. The community rebounded to more than 300 people during the 2000s.

As the town fights for its survival, the school seems to have become the epicenter of Bluejacket. Located a few short blocks from Main Street, the school serves hundreds of students in kindergarten through twelfth grade.

McHone, for one, still raves about the town he calls beautiful and all that it offers to those who remain. "For the most part, the town is kept pretty clean. It's a great place and, I think, safe. I don't lock my house. I don't ever lock my house. My garage is open. My neighbor needs something, he goes and gets it and brings it back."

Creek County

Burnett Mansion

320 South Main Street, Sapulpa

When Bates Burnett moved to this oil boom city southwest of Tulsa from North Carolina, he—like many others—had grand visions about the home he would build along one of Sapulpa's busiest streets as a way to show the wealth he had amassed over the years. Following his marriage to Dannie Ross, a descendant of the Cherokee Indian chief John Ross, the couple spent three years building their opulent dream home.

The couple spared no expense to build the southern plantation–style home. Architects from New York were hired to draw up the blueprints, while woodwork from Spain and Portugal and lavish stained-glass windows and fixtures were imported.

"They wanted the best of the best at that time period," said Scarlett Firey, who, along with her parents, owns and offers tours of the historical Main Street home.

Work on the home, which includes six bedrooms and a third-floor ballroom, was completed in 1911 at a cost of $85,000, Firey said. Back then, Sapulpa was filled with oil-rich men and their families, eager to show off their growing wealth. Burnett chose Main Street for his home as a sign of prestige. "The Main Street was a lot different back then, and I think they were very showy people and wanted to be socialites in town, and they wanted everyone to drive by and see what they had built and created."

Today, the 6,500-square-foot mansion is surrounded by commercial businesses and developments that have popped up along Main Street.

The Burnett Mansion in Sapulpa, Oklahoma, in Creek County.

Bates Burnett died in 1925, but family members remained in the home until the 1980s. Once Bates died, the Burnett family became very private, Firey said, and let few people into the home. Their reclusiveness, however, helped preserve the historical elements of the mansion.

"The thing about the home is that it's been taken care of really well," Firey said. "The Burnetts, once their father died, they didn't change anything in the home, so it basically stayed as is until the late eighties."

Bates Burnett's daughter, Katherine, was the last family member to remain in the home. She died in 1984, and the house was sold at an auction to Marcia and Ronald Warren, who worked hard to repair the foundation and give the home a good top-to-bottom scrubbing after years of decay.

"When we bought the house, it was so dirty that we hired ten or twenty workers to help us clean the house," Marcia Warren told the *Oklahoman* newspaper in 1984. "We worked nearly ten hours a day for about ten days. I've never cleaned so hard in my life."

The Fireys purchased the home in 2007 and are the fourth owners since Katherine's death. It's primarily used as a commercial property for various events like weddings, parties and receptions. The home is opened for private tours by request.

A new feature further transforms the home for visitors interested in a snapshot of years past. Called Miss Scarlett's Tea Room, the restaurant serving sandwiches and bakery items takes people back to what it was like when afternoons revolved around teatime. "We have a lot of people that want inside for tours and history of the home, and before, we would just do the tours and send them on down the road," Firey said. But now people "can stop and enjoy it a little longer than the quick tour."

Custer County

Western Oklahoma Historical Center

520 West Main Street, Weatherford

On the western edge of Main Street in this city of about eleven thousand people—past the boutiques and restaurants lining historic Route 66—sit roomfuls of history. The Western Plains Weatherford Genealogical Society and the Western Oklahoma Historical Center are located just a few blocks north of city hall.

The genealogical library, located in a former house, contains more than eight hundred rolls of microfilm, most of them from Oklahoma, and a large collection of obituaries dating back to the 1890s, said Laura McCormick, research coordinator. The genealogy library was originally located in the public library, but when it outgrew the library's space, it moved in the early 2000s to the home along Main Street.

The all-volunteer staff at the library and research center helps visitors research their family trees, something McCormick believes everyone should know about.

"If we don't know the history of this part of the country, of the United States, we are going to lose what our forefathers came over for, and basically most of them came here for religious freedom," McCormick said.

Having researched her own family history, McCormick said she wasn't just interested in who her great-great-grandparents were but what they were about—what they did for a living and what struggles they may have endured.

Next door to the genealogy library and research center sits the Cedar Schoolhouse, a one-room school originally located northwest of Weatherford but relocated following its closing in the 1950s. The schoolhouse takes

The Cedar Schoolhouse, a one-room school, located along Main Street in Weatherford, Oklahoma.

The famed Route 66 is also known as Main Street in Weatherford, Oklahoma.

visitors back to a different time, when schools were located within four miles of one another so no student had to walk more than two miles to attend, said McCormick. Inkwells sit at each desk, and a chair is connected to the front of the desk. Every August, former students who attended Cedar gather at the one-room school and reminisce.

"Of course [the gatherings are] getting thinner and thinner because it hasn't been open in quite a while," McCormick said.

McCormick said the two groups—the Western Plains Weatherford Genealogical Society and the Western Oklahoma Historical Center—remain separate nonprofit entities but work closely together. About eight hundred to one thousand people visit the schoolhouse and genealogy library each year.

Delaware County

Huckleberry Festival Parade

Main Street, Jay

For a few days in July, the approximately 2,500 residents of the northeastern Oklahoma city of Jay gather together to celebrate the deliciousness of the huckleberry—the small, round berry that is often blue or black and is similar to a blueberry. Known locally as the "Huckleberry Capital of the World," Jay has been hosting a Huckleberry Festival since 1967.

"It's one of our major events. It's a fun time for families to come together and enjoy each other," said Jackie Coatney, curator of the Delaware County Historical Society and Marie Wallace Museum, as well as secretary of the chamber of commerce, which sponsors the festival.

The festival, typically around the July Fourth holiday, has events all over the city, but the parade takes place along Main Street and starts promptly at 10:00 a.m.

People may come from all over the state for the festival and the homegrown huckleberries, but it's up to Mother Nature to determine how well it turns out. "Basically, we rely upon Mother Nature to give us the berries," said Coatney, noting that some years turn out well while others aren't as great.

In addition to the parade, the festival features a car show, pancake breakfast, 5K run, arts and crafts and several options for enjoying the sweet-tasting fruit—as part of a winning pie, as syrup atop a fluffy pancake, as a milkshake or as a topping on a bowl of vanilla ice cream in the town square.

For the residents of Jay, it's a time to come together to celebrate the town and its unique history. Jay is the county seat of Delaware County, but it wasn't always. It took over the title after a hard-fought battle with the

Main Street in Jay, Oklahoma.

citizens of Grove, about twelve miles to the north, which was the county seat when Oklahoma became a state in 1907. Fed up with having to travel more than thirty miles to get to the courthouse in Grove in the northern edge of the county, a group of residents in the southern portion formed a group to try to move the county seat to a more central location. A town site was platted, and a special election was held to move the seat to a new area named Jay. County residents voted in favor of having Jay as the county seat, but residents of Grove weren't going down without a fight. They appealed to the Oklahoma Supreme Court, and a years-long court battle ensued—along with the repeated transferring of court records between the courthouses in Grove and Jay and a third courthouse that had been built—before Jay was known as the rightful winner of the title of county seat. Today, the county courthouse is located just south of Main Street in the town's main business district.

Dewey County

Veterans Memorial Park

Corner of Main and Third Streets, Seiling

It's not every day that a military tanker is pulled down a Main Street in Oklahoma. But that's exactly what happened in the early 1990s as organizers in this city of 860 people in the northwestern portion of the state worked to assemble a new Veterans Memorial Park.

The tanker that ended up as a main focal point in the park dedicated to the former members of the armed forces didn't exactly arrive at its desired location easily. The army donated the tanker, as it tends to do for such projects, but once it arrived in town, it wouldn't come off the truck, said Seiling resident Dava Carter. Her husband, Butch Carter, had to use a tractor to pull the monstrous combat vehicle and put it in place.

"It was pretty funny," Dava Carter said of watching her Vietnam veteran husband jockey the tanker into place.

Eventually, the tank was steered to its desired position, surrounded by a three-sided enclosure made up of bricks listing the names of veterans from the area. Each person paid twenty-five dollars to get his name on a brick on the wall, which was laid by some of the veterans who were also skilled at masonry. In front of the brick wall stand three rifles with their barrel ends all leaning into each other, forming an upside-down V. On the tips sits a single military helmet, a touching tribute to the many veterans who fought for the country's freedoms. It's exactly what organizers of the park wanted.

Visitors to Seiling, Oklahoma, will see a military tank on Main Street.

A veterans memorial is located along Main Street in Seiling, Oklahoma.

"It's a reminder to everyone of the sacrifices people have made for the country, and it also provides a place that people going through see it and stop and look," Dava Carter said.

But what about fears of a possible late-night joy ride down Main Street in the tanker? Carter said that shouldn't be a concern; the hulking military vehicle has been adjusted so it can't run.

Ellis County

Shattuck Windmill Museum and Park

Eleventh Street and Main Street, Shattuck

There are tall ones and short ones, fat ones and skinny ones. There are old ones and then really, really old ones. Though some may look similar, no two are the same. The dozens of windmills that stand at the park on the corner of Main and Eleventh Streets in Shattuck come from all over the Great Plains of the United States and catch the eyes of passing motorists.

The Shattuck Windmill Museum and Park, established in 1994 and dedicated two years later, pays tribute to the machine that was once integral to the livelihood of every homesteader arriving in western Oklahoma. "Out here, unlike a lot of other areas in the country, other areas have running water and streams and stuff. Out here it's far and few between, so you've got to get water out of the ground," said Jim Schoenhals, secretary of the museum's board of directors. "Well, the windmill made that possible. And that's the key. Without the windmill, this place would be undeveloped."

As a child, Phillis Ballew was used to her mother chiding her for climbing onto the family windmill at their house. Years later, Ballew once again found herself fascinated with the machine. This time, though, she was looking at it as a way to draw visitors to the community of 1,300 in northwest Oklahoma, and she became one of the founders of the museum and park made up of more than sixty windmills.

On an unseasonably warm winter day, Ballew walks through the park, maneuvering through the various machines, some more than one hundred years old, and recounts details of how each of them came to reside in

Phillis Ballew stands in front of a windmill at the Shattuck Windmill Museum and Park in Shattuck, Oklahoma.

Shattuck, including the Railroad Eclipse, which at eighteen feet is the tallest of the mills.

Some of the most rare and oldest windmills have been moved inside to a new building on the property to keep them safe from the outside elements. The museum volunteers hope to replace one of the sides of the buildings with glass so visitors can peer inside to see the old windmills whenever they want.

Because the museum founders wanted to bring to life old-time Oklahoma, a small dug-out sod house and a homestead house are also a part of the windmill park. The sod house, or soddy as it's sometimes known, was originally located a few miles outside of Shattuck but was moved and reconstructed on the museum and park land. A table and chairs, tiny bed with quilt and kitchenware inside the quaint sod house demonstrate what life was like back when the home was built in 1904.

Nearby, another neatly manicured yellow home with white trimming and a front porch showcases what a family might have lived in once they left a soddy. The one-and-a-half-story home was built around 1900 and has a living and dining room, bedroom and a very narrow stairway leading up to an attic that housed the children's quarters.

Out front at the park, visitors can see the George Schultz General Merchandise Store, a reconstruction of a 1904 store that was originally on Main Street. Today, it houses books, postcards, windmill jewelry and other memorabilia that aficionados of windmills or Oklahoma history may want to buy.

Garfield County

Garber-Billings News

516 Main Street, Garber

In a tiny, nondescript building with wood shingles, two windows in front and an American flag flying outside, Lacey Deeds single-handedly produces what can require, in some instances, groups of people to do: a community newspaper full of the weekly achievements, announcements and performances of the community's approximately 825 residents.

With no previous journalism experience or background, Deeds purchased the weekly *Garber-Billings News* after its previous owner suddenly passed away from a heart attack on Christmas Day in 2012.

"The paper was going to close, and so I purchased it from the family because the paper has been in production for 114 years," she said.

Garber at one time had two newspapers, but today the *Garber-Billings News* is the sole media outlet covering both Garber and Billings, a community of about five hundred people about fifteen miles away in Noble County. But with less ink in the community, the newspaper, which has a circulation of about five hundred, may be valued even more.

One former resident, Deeds said, recently called her up to show his appreciation for what she does. After graduating more than fifty years ago from Garber schools and moving away, the man, who had no family ties to the community, subscribed to the paper in order to keep up with his former community and the grandkids of his one-time classmates who are now featured all over the newspaper's pages.

"He still loves the paper and staying connected that way," said Deeds, thirty-eight, who moved to Garber when she was about ten years old.

The *Garber-Billings News* in Garber, Oklahoma.

Deeds has taken a hands-on approach to her new role, making it very easy for people to share their tips for news stories even when she's not in the office. Her email, office phone and cell phone numbers are listed on the door of the *Garber-Billings News* building on Main Street.

But don't expect any controversial stories or investigative journalism about the local officials across the street at city hall. Deeds prefers to keep the newspaper filled with positive and uplifting news. "Nothing negative is ever published in my paper. It's all good stuff," Deeds said. "We want to build the communities up. We don't want to tear them down. We grew up in the paper and our kids grew up in the paper, and that's what people look for. They want to open the paper and feel good. I don't like negativity."

Instead, Deeds likes to focus on what the local children are up to and what events are taking place in the communities, which she said are full of welcoming residents and long-lasting traditions.

"We keep things going on that have been going on for years," Deeds said of Garber and Billings.

The land that would become Garber was opened for settlement by a land run in September 1893. Milton Garber, who was a lawyer and would later become a judge, newspaper publisher and member of the United States House of Representatives, and his brother, Burton A. Garber, president of the Farmers State Bank and the Garber and Company store, platted the town near where their father had homesteaded.

For the foreseeable future, Deeds, a mother of three, will be giving a voice to the area through her newspaper. "I'm just a mom, a 4-H leader that didn't want the paper to go away, so I just jumped in with both feet."

Garvin County

Tammy Briggs, Owner of Ms. Tammy's Parlor and Salon

211 South Main Street, Elmore City

This town has a lot of wonderful, great, giving people, and the churches are real strong. I would never go hungry or starve. I'd always have a place to live, and I know that.
—Tammy Briggs

Briggs has a love-hate relationship with Elmore City, a town of fewer than seven hundred people in south-central Oklahoma. The fifty-three-year-old mother of four moved to the area nearly thirty years ago with her husband. The two aren't together anymore, but Briggs, meanwhile, has stayed put in Elmore City, which is most famous for being the inspiration for the film *Footloose*, which based its plot on events that happened in 1980 in the small town.

Elmore City, Briggs said, is a place where everybody knows everybody's business, which can be both a blessing and a curse.

"At first...I literally thought I'd died and gone to hell," Briggs said, recalling how she felt when she first moved to the area. "When I first came here, I was leery because it seemed like a dump town, like it was where everybody dumped people that they didn't want to raise anymore."

Slowly, though, the town has grown on her.

When she went through tough times, the town's people rallied behind her and helped her out, she said. Other business owners cancelled debts and helped her find a new place to stay with her children.

It's also where she has operated several different businesses: a daycare, a tanning salon, an aerobics class and, now, a hair salon.

Ms. Tammy's Parlor and Salon in Elmore City, Oklahoma.

Ms. Tammy's Parlor and Salon was originally located on a residential street, but in 2011, she bought a building on Main Street to increase traffic.

In a small community, there are lots of opportunities for gossip, Briggs said, but it's not welcome in her salon.

"When you walk in here, it's home. It's just family. Everyone is family here," she said. In fact, she jokes, everyone is family—literally. Living in a small town means most people are related in one way or another, so it's important to be careful about what you say.

Originally from Oklahoma City, Briggs said she now finds comfort in her small town. She enjoys walking around the building that houses her salon for exercise and often walks across the street to a bank for change.

"I don't even have to have the right names on checks. People write all kinds of weird names on my checks and I can just cash them, because I just know the people," she said.

In April 2013, Briggs got married for the third time—and in a unique way. Briggs and her husband married at the Footloose Festival, an event along the town's Main Street to commemorate the town's tie to the famous film. It was the first time a couple had gotten married at the festival.

Ms. Tammy's Parlor and Salon in Elmore City, Oklahoma.

"We didn't have to have a wedding," she said of why they chose to tie the knot in such a distinctive way. "We didn't have to have a party, because there were two dances going on. We thought, what better way to get married? We don't have to buy a cake. We don't have to invite people. They're already all here, and there was a big dance afterward."

The plot of the 1984 movie, starring Kevin Bacon, is loosely based on events in Elmore City. In 1980, the graduating high school class got permission to dance at the prom, lifting a nearly one-hundred-year-old ban.

Grady County

Neoma McKinney, Owner of Neoma's This and That Thrift Store and More

309 West Main Street, Tuttle

People just look for stores like this because we're all kind of junkers I've found out.
—*Neoma McKinney*

Neoma McKinney loves meeting people on the job. First it was while working at a bank, and then later she met people young and old while operating a convenience store along Tuttle's Main Street. When the city bought her store to make room for a brand-new city hall, McKinney turned her attention to her other love: making homemade jams, jellies and salsas.

Initially only selling them at the local farmers' market, McKinney decided in June 2012 to finally make use of the building she had bought years before along Main Street—just down the street from where her convenience store was—and turn it into a thrift store selling a variety of items, including her famous jams, jellies and salsas.

"I got so close to people at that convenience store—the kids, the parents. I was there for eight years, and actually what I like about it [opening the new thrift store] is being back on Main Street and seeing a lot of customers from the bank, customers from my convenience store," the seventy-four-year-old said.

The job is also nice, McKinney said, because it's stress free. "I have the key to the front door—not that I take off any, but if I need to I don't have to come and do this. And when you don't have to do it, you enjoy it more."

Although the store is fairly new, it's very familiar to McKinney. When she was in high school, she worked in the restaurant that was housed in part of the building. The other half was a barbershop at the time.

Neoma's This and That Thrift Store and More in Tuttle, Oklahoma.

Neoma McKinney stands next to her jellies and jams in her store along Main Street in Tuttle, Oklahoma.

Today, there's not even a sit-down restaurant to eat breakfast at along Main Street, McKinney noted, but it doesn't matter. Tuttle and its six thousand residents will always be home for her.

"You get to know all these people," McKinney said of life owning a business in a small town. "It's just awesome to know your neighbors and the people across town and the people out in the country. It's just what I enjoy rather than living somewhere I may know my next-door neighbor and that's all."

McKinney has watched as the high school students she once served at the convenience store have turned into adults, gotten married and had their own children. And the Tuttle school system, McKinney said, is one of the best things about the town, and many of her customers in her store with kids say it's the reason they moved to the area.

So where do the customers come from who visit her store? Both near and far. Some are local residents who swear by her salsa, which comes in medium and hot, and twenty-two flavors of jams and jellies. Other customers are people taking Oklahoma back roads who happen upon the town in northern Grady County, about thirty miles southwest of Oklahoma City. And still others stop by This and That to and from tours at the nearby Braum's ice cream bakery and processing plant in Tuttle.

Grant County

Twister Museum

101 West Main Street, Wakita

The 1996 Hollywood blockbuster *Twister* put the blink-and-you-miss-it town of Wakita on the map—by pretending to wipe it off.

Though Oklahomans have long been accustomed to the severe weather that wallops the state every spring, the film—which tells the story of a group of storm chasers trying to get their data-gathering equipment inside the funnel of a tornado—brought greater attention to tornadoes and their devastating effects.

In the movie, Wakita was decimated by an F-4 tornado, but in real life, the rubble and havoc left in the tornado's wake was all thanks to some Hollywood special effects mastery and planning. Producers built sets along Main Street in Wakita, population 344, depicting the fronts of buildings. The sets, along with a few buildings already in the process of being torn down, were then demolished by the "destruction" of the tornado.

When production wrapped in Oklahoma on the film in the summer of 1995, Linda Wade and others opened up the *Twister* Museum in the film's former location office on Main Street.

Though attendance at the museum has dropped off since it first opened nearly twenty years ago, regular visitors are still drawn to the compact museum brimming with photographs, memorabilia and the original Dorothy 1 measuring device seen in the film. Visitors can also see a pinball machine donated by Bill Paxton, one of the film's stars, and home videos of the filming. An Oklahoma City Thunder jersey also hangs in the former movie office in honor of star player Kevin Durant, who is a fan of *Twister*.

The original Dorothy 1 from the movie *Twister* can be seen at the *Twister* Museum along Main Street in Wakita, Oklahoma.

About three to four different groups or individuals visit the museum each day when the museum is open in the spring and summer, Wade said. Severe weather can bring even bigger crowds—storm chasers are known to stop by and show off their new equipment and compare it to Dorothy 1.

"As far as we're concerned, three or four visitors during the day in the summertime is quite a few when you have zero visitors before that," Wade said. "We're quite happy to have that many visitors each day. It's put Wakita on the map for sure."

Greer County

Large Guitar Sculpture

Main Street between Fourth Street and Parker Avenue, Granite

Granite may be a sleepy town nestled at the base of Headquarters Mountain, but its rockin' musical history is celebrated in a twelve-foot-tall guitar statue placed unassumingly in a park along Main Street.

There are no markers or signs explaining why a guitar statue ended up in between two buildings and just a few steps from the city hall. Ask a local in town and they might not know, either. But if you do enough asking, you'll learn the artwork was to celebrate a time when the town was home to a guitar institute run by a family of well-known classical guitarists.

Jimmy Ammons, a local mechanic known for being covered in grease and dirt and writing articles for the local newspaper, created the guitar using various pieces from items considered historical, like an antique combine.

The sculpture was built to celebrate Granite hosting the inaugural Celedonio Romero Guitar Institute in conjunction with the now-defunct Quartz Mountain Music Festival. Celedonio was an acclaimed Spanish guitarist in the mid-twentieth century who recruited his sons to form a quartet. Together, the Romeros, which now includes a third generation, perform around the world, including recitals at the White House and the Vatican. The idea behind the institute was to give college students an opportunity to learn classical guitar from some of the best, said Brenda Hickerson, who was on the board of the Quartz Mountain Music Festival.

"The entire event was an excellent example of small-town collaboration to bring an event like this to our little town in southwest Oklahoma," Hickerson said. The Granite School donated its facilities for lessons and

Jimmy Ammons stands next to the twelve-foot-tall guitar he made in Granite, Oklahoma. *Courtesy of Willis Granite Products.*

practice sessions; churches hosted and donated lunches and dinners; and local residents opened up their homes to the musicians playing the festival.

Regrettably, the community spirit was not enough to keep the institute or the music festival alive in Granite, population 2,065, and both shuttered, with the institute moving to Southern Nazarene University in Bethany. The sculpture was moved to Main Street in remembrance of the educational experiment and the town's efforts to become a musical destination.

Harmon County

Old Greer County Historical Marker

Corner of Main and Hollis Streets, Hollis

Back in the late 1800s, standing at the corner of what is now Main and Hollis Streets meant you were in Texas, not in Oklahoma or Oklahoma Territory. The land was part of Greer County, Texas, up until the United States Supreme Court ruled in 1896 that Greer County should be handed over from Texas to Oklahoma Territory. After Oklahoma became a state in 1907, Harmon County was formed from a portion of Greer County, and Hollis became the county seat.

All told, the area was claimed by fourteen different governments from 1669 to when Oklahoma became a state. It's enough to leave a visitor dizzy with details. To help keep it straight, a historical marker was placed outside the Harmon County Courthouse.

The marker, placed by the Oklahoma Historical Society and State Highway Commission in 1954, notes the county's changing name and history.

Located in extreme southwest Oklahoma, Harmon County is isolated, making it the second-least-populated county in Oklahoma, only trailing Cimarron County in the Panhandle. The county was named for Judson C. Harmon, who was the United States attorney when Old Greer County was opened for settlement.

Main Street in Hollis, population two thousand, runs north and south. Though the east–west street of Broadway is the city's main artery, Main Street is home to the middle and high schools, city hall and jail, county courthouse and several homes.

Harper County

Jane Jayroe, Namesake for Renaming Main Street to Jane Jayroe Boulevard, Laverne

Like many communities in western Oklahoma large and small, the prime road through Laverne was for decades known simply as Main Street. But all that changed in the late 1960s, when a local girl made every small-town girl's dream a reality: she became Miss America.

Jane Jayroe didn't grow up in Laverne, but she soon grew to love it. The town and its people would soon grow to love Jayroe, too, and to show their appreciation, Main Street was renamed Jane Jayroe Boulevard after she was crowned Miss America in 1967.

"It was such a beautiful gesture," the former Miss America said. "I'm still overwhelmed by that reality and hope they don't regret it as the years go on."

Jayroe was born in Clinton, Oklahoma, in 1947 and moved with her parents to Sentinel, a tiny town in west-central Oklahoma, when she was two years old. Sentinel is where her dad grew up and where some of her extended family lived. The family remained there until right before Jayroe's freshman year of high school. That's when they moved to the "big town" of Laverne, a scary transition for a girl who was shy and had only remembered living in one place her whole life. With seventy-three students, the high school class was triple the size of Sentinel's and had a greater selection of after-school activities, including football and marching band.

Any apprehension she felt was soon replaced by excitement, however. The larger class size that had at one time scared Jayroe, in fact, offered her a chance to get to know gifted students in academics, athletics and leadership.

Jayroe played on the girls' basketball team, which lost only a handful of games during her four years in high school.

In 1966, while a student at Oklahoma City University, she won the Miss Oklahoma City pageant and the Miss Oklahoma pageant, clearing the way for her to compete in the Miss America pageant. With little experience in the world of bathing suits, big hair, big smiles and big dreams of the pageant world, Jayroe was as shocked as anybody else that she beat out the other women and won the title of Miss America.

"I was so young and inexperienced and insecure," she said of the time that was initially unsettling. "But soon, by the grace of God, I was able to live into that role and experience the change of a lifetime."

Quickly adapting to the demands of the new role, Jayroe traveled to nearly every state in the United States as well as Canada and Europe and performed in Vietnam to support American troops. "I participated in such a variety of events—it was an education of a decade," she recalls years later.

Following her reign, Jayroe went on to become a news reporter and anchor and served as the secretary of tourism in Oklahoma. She now lives in Oklahoma City with her husband and is an author and volunteer and runs a luncheon focused on faith for women.

Though the trips to Laverne, which celebrated its centennial in 2013, have become less frequent for Jayroe following her mother's death, she still looks back fondly on the community of 1,300 people and says the values she learned growing up there—an appreciation for people from all walks of life, a love of country, strong faith in God, a focus on family and a love of community—helped shape her and her notable career.

Haskell County

Haskell County Courthouse

202 East Main Street, Stigler

The battle over the First Amendment and the separation of church and state brewed for several years in this community of two thousand in eastern Oklahoma. Michael Bush, a construction worker and part-time minister, asked the three-county board of commissioners for its approval to place an eight-foot-tall Ten Commandments monument on the lawn of the Haskell County Courthouse in Stigler.

Saying the "Lord had burdened [his] heart" to erect the statue, Bush, after receiving approval from the board, raised money to build the monument. In addition to the Ten Commandments, Bush decided to inscribe the Mayflower Compact on the statue as well.

In November 2004, the large structure was placed just off Main Street—the town's main thoroughfare, which is also State Highway 9—near monuments honoring citizens killed in World Wars I and II and the Choctaw Nation. A dedication ceremony drew a few hundred people, several local churches and two of the three commissioners—as well as an onslaught of media attention as reporters and others wondered about the religious symbol on public property. Despite the controversy, the commissioners stood by their decision, with one commissioner quoted as saying about the Ten Commandments, "That's what we're trying to live by, that right there…The good Lord died for me. I can stand for him, and I'm going to…I'm a Christian, and I believe in this. I think it's a benefit to the community."

Nearly a year later, the American Civil Liberties Union, ACLU of Oklahoma and local resident James W. Green filed suit against the monument, saying it was unconstitutional. The United States District Court for the Eastern District of Oklahoma ruled against the ACLU and Green in 2006, but the plaintiffs appealed to the United States Tenth Circuit Court of Appeals. That court reversed the decision, saying a Ten Commandment statute on a courthouse lawn is unconstitutional because it reflects the government endorsing a religion.

The United States Supreme Court in 2010 decided to let stand the Tenth Circuit Court's decision ruling the monument unconstitutional. But people don't have to go far to see the statue that divided the community for several years. Following the Supreme Court's decision not to get involved, the eight-foot monument was moved about a block away from the courthouse to private property.

Hughes County

Sucker Day Festival

Main Street, Wetumka

When F. Bam Morrison strolled into this east-central Oklahoma community in July 1950, he had news to share with its residents: a circus would be coming to town in a few short weeks. Morrison's job as the advance man for the traveling show called Bohn's United Circus was to plan and complete all the tasks in preparation for the show's arrival.

Or so the people of Wetumka thought.

In a story for the *Henryettan*, Earl Goldsmith wrote about how Morrison sought out Boy Scouts to sell tickets, reserved grounds for the performances and rooms at a local hotel for promoters and had local grocery stores and restaurants stock up on extra items to feed the planned circus-goers. Morrison also sold and placed signs around Wetumka for the countless tourists who were expected to converge on the area for the performances, scheduled for July 24–25, 1950, according to Goldsmith.

"By the middle of July, he completed his arrangements and left to make arrangements for the next circus stop. Wetumkans were waiting for the circus with an unusual amount of excitement," Goldsmith wrote.

Right before the performances were scheduled to start, a few incredulous residents began to suspect something was amiss. For starters, there was no equipment for a circus and no employees to run it. But ever the optimists, the community's residents lined up along Main Street on the morning of July 24, eager to watch the parade that would mark the elaborate circus's arrival.

The parade never happened. Neither did a circus, and residents quickly realized Morrison had duped them. Rather than become bitter, though, the

Main Street in Wetumka, Oklahoma.

The Sucker Day parade in Wetumka, Oklahoma.

people of Wetumka decided to make the best of a rotten event by holding their own celebration, complete with concessions and street dancing. "Sucker Day" has become an annual affair, a reminder of how community members didn't let a bad guy and a sour situation ruin their fun.

Hundreds of people from all over the area now gather each year on the last Saturday in September on Main Street in the city of 1,280 to watch a parade featuring local marching bands, consume too many sugary snacks and mingle with friends and family.

Jackson County

Belles and Beaux

116 North Main Street, Altus

As a child, I always remembered that the stores had always used to be down on the square, so that's where I wanted to be. I wanted to be more in a family-type setting, and that's why I opened here.
—Krystal Martin, owner of Belles and Beaux

Krystal Martin had never really planned to open a children's clothing store or get into the retail business at all. Sure, she had two young boys and often stopped and shopped for clothes at the children's store along Main Street, just across from the Jackson County Courthouse, but the thought of owning a clothing store for kids never really crossed her mind.

What did appeal to her was what her husband had—a flexible schedule, the ability to be his own boss and an interesting career field.

So, in the late 1990s, when Martin got the chance to take over the children's store she had once shopped in, she jumped for it. Instead of going to their out-of-business sale to buy clothes, Martin said, she ended up with fixtures and equipment. A few months later, Belles and Beaux was born in Altus, a city of 19,800 in southwestern Oklahoma.

The store features clothes for both boys and girls, all the way from preemie sizes to child sizes, as well as gifts and older-style toys.

The toys at Belles and Beaux will be a trip down memory lane for many of the parents who may have used Lincoln Logs to build miniature forts and buildings or competed with friends over the game of pick-up sticks.

"We do baby registries. We do baby bedding. We do a lot of toys—specialty toys and unique products that you don't find anywhere else," the forty-six-year-old Martin said.

Upon deciding to give a go at running a children's store, Martin knew she had to open up her store in the same location along Main Street. "I knew through the years so many people would remember that the east side of the square always had a children's store," she said. "So I felt not only would it be beneficial to start there, if nothing else, people may or may not realize that that one store had closed and a new one had opened up, and at least I'd be in the same location."

About eight years ago, Martin bought a second store—called the Booterie, which, you guessed it, sells shoes—that is located just two doors down from Belles and Beaux, also on Main Street. "It's kind of one of those historic icons that everybody always refers to and says, 'You know, it's down there next to the Booterie,'" she said. "It's almost a landmark."

Both stores keep Martin busy, especially lately because the markets for buying stock for both are in different places—inventory for the shoe store is purchased in Atlanta, while the children's clothing is usually obtained in Dallas.

But, she said, despite the travel, owning the two stores and being her own boss is enjoyable. She also employs a full-time manager as well as two part-time employees at Belles and Beaux to help her out. It's good she does, because Main Street and the historic square have seen a period of rapid growth in recent years. There are no vacancies around the square, and many businesses that once moved out are returning, creating an air of excitement for the business community, she said.

"A lot of people are really realizing now, due to the downturn in the economy...people are actually starting to see that shopping in town, that money stays in town and those sales-tax dollars stay in town and they help fund things like our police, our fire department and our city employees that are now being laid off."

Jefferson County

Fangtastic Waurika Rattlesnake Hunt

Main Street, Waurika

The scaly, slithering creatures with razor-sharp fangs and dangerous venom strike fear in the hearts and minds of many. But for the residents of this southern Oklahoma city, the rattlesnake is anything but frightening. In fact, the reptile has been bringing the community together for decades.

The Fangtastic Waurika Rattlesnake Hunt draws gawkers, adventurers and other curious-minded folks from across the nation to see and experience rattlesnakes up close. The three-day event held during the second weekend of April each year raises money for Waurika's volunteer fire department.

"You know, it's something different. A lot of people have never had the opportunity to go to something like that," said volunteer firefighter Brandon Austin.

The main event, of course, is the search for the wriggling snakes, with prizes awarded for people in different categories, including longest snake or the snake with the most rattles. The hunt typically takes place in the early afternoon along the banks of the nearby Red River. As the rattlers are coming out of their dens to warm up, the hunters use tongs—or, if they're feeling especially brave, hooks—to snag the scaly creatures.

It seems like an unsafe endeavor, but Austin, who regularly takes part in the hunt, doesn't seemed fazed by it. Bites, he said, aren't too much of a concern, either.

For those who think hunting the snakes is too daunting, there's another option: eating them.

The chance to eat snake meat, described as light and chewy and similar in taste to—what else?—chicken, is another draw that keeps people coming to Waurika, population 2,060. "A lot of people come for it, yes, and some people just want to come and try it. We sell a lot of it," Austin said.

On Main Street, a carnival with rides, a flea market and vendors selling a variety of items offer some respite for those weary of rattlers.

The hunt originally started back in 1961 as a way to control the overabundance of snakes slithering through the community. It soon became a fun-filled family event that raises on average about $35,000 for the fire department, which goes toward buying new equipment, Austin said.

Despite the annual hunt, Austin said the rattlesnake population can still be problematic in certain areas, meaning the hunt for the venomous reptiles will probably be around for years to come.

Johnson County

The Pink Pistol

214 West Main Street, Tishomingo

Cowboy boots and jeans have long been a staple of life in Tishomingo, the county seat of Johnson County and the one-time capital of the Chickasaw Nation. They are typical pieces of clothing worn by many who stroll along Main Street. In recent years, however, the typical bland brown boots and well-worn blue jeans have taken a back seat to shiny sparkles, elaborate laces and bright hues of pink and purple that have added some glitz to the average country-style woman's wardrobe.

And that's just what country superstar Miranda Lambert had in mind when she opened the Pink Pistol in her adopted hometown of Tishomingo in 2012.

Described by Lambert as a store for the "wild at heart," Pink Pistol is stocked full of women's clothing, books by fellow country mavens and an assortment of trinkets and jewelry items. Though originally born in Texas, Lambert calls Tishomingo home when not crisscrossing the country performing for her many adoring fans. She decided to open up her store in the community of three thousand because, she said, it's the epitome of a great, small town in America.

People from near and far pop into the store that features a sign with a giant pink pistol with wings outside. It's easy to glean that pink is the Grammy-winning musician's favorite color. The store is awash in pink details, like a large pink horse statue that sits in the window.

In addition to cowboy boots, T-shirts, jeans, scarves, moccasins and other clothing items, the Pink Pistol also stocks some kitchenware, accessories and

Pink Pistol in Tishomingo features sequins, cowboy boots and, of course, plenty of pink.

books written by other famous ladies with Oklahoma ties, including fellow country singer Trisha Yearwood, who is married to Oklahoma native Garth Brooks, and Ree Drummond, better known as the Pioneer Woman.

An old-fashioned sundae shop located at the front of the store sells sundaes and floats and makes any trip to the Pink Pistol extra sweet. Lambert, who has won numerous awards from the Country Music Association and the Academy of Country Music for songs including "Over You" and "The House That Built Me," and the store host an annual Pink Friday on the day after Thanksgiving with live music and vendors.

Kay County

Top of Oklahoma Museum

303 South Main Street, Blackwell

Everywhere you look in one of the compact rooms within the Top of the Oklahoma Museum, a doll stares back. The more than one thousand dolls come in various shapes and sizes and facial expressions, filling the small room to the brim.

The doll collection is just one trove of items at this museum dedicated to preserving and sharing the story of Blackwell, a city of a little more than seven thousand residents fewer than twenty miles south of the Kansas border established in 1893 by a Georgia transplant named A.J. Blackwell.

The town's history is seen through thousands of pieces throughout the museum—from clothing to dishes, a cane collection and pianos. Various rooms are set up to focus on one topic, including the military room, which features information about what to do in time of war and natural disasters. A collection of photographs depicts what Blackwell looked like following a deadly tornado in 1955, while a room filled with medical equipment tells the stories of some of the area's most well-known healthcare professionals.

Nearby, a small room contains Native American items, including a replica tipi, moccasins, photographs and beadwork. The room is a salute to the county's historical ties to American Indians. Kay County was originally part of the strip of land given to Cherokee Indians to use for hunting grounds before the United States government took it away as a penalty for some of the tribal members fighting with the Southern Confederates in the Civil War.

The land was designated as county "K," and that's how the county is still known today, albeit with a different spelling.

The Top of Oklahoma Museum in the Electric Park Pavilion in Blackwell, Oklahoma.

At the intersection of Main Street and Oklahoma Avenue in Blackwell, Oklahoma.

Old records dating back decades such as yearbooks and civil and social organizations are used by would-be genealogists searching for family history. A more damaging part of history is recorded in a box full of membership cards from the Ku Klux Klan.

The museum is housed in the Electric Park Pavilion, a grand structure that opened in 1913 to pay tribute to electricity. With more than five hundred lights illuminating the building and its dome, the structure could be seen for miles.

Kingfisher County

Garden's Edge

107 South Main Street, Hennessey

Housed in a former bank building that is now listed on the National Register of Historic Places, Garden's Edge bills itself as the hometown flower shop of Hennessey, a community of about 2,100 in north-central Kingfisher County.

The brainchild of three local women, the shop opened in 1999 in the more than one-hundred-year-old Farmers and Merchants Bank building and quickly became the go-to place for locals and visitors to buy floral arrangements, candles and an assortment of other gifts.

But, owner Donna Haymaker said, the store is much more than a flower and gift shop. It's also a place where people can sit back, relax and take the time to eat a light meal of homemade soups, salads and sandwiches before returning to the hustle and bustle of everyday life.

Garden's Edge seats as many as thirty people for lunch in the front of the store. Some days the place will be filled with people. Other days, though, the store is lucky to have a few lunch ladies. But that's what Haymaker and her sister-in-law anticipated when they opened the store. "We knew in a small town we couldn't make enough money on a flower shop to pay the bills," she said.

Haymaker, who studied art at a nearby university, never dreamed she would get into the floral business—and it hasn't been easy. Making sure there's enough cash flow and enough advertising to draw people into the store are the big worries. Luckily, social media and email have made marketing easier.

The Farmers and Merchants Bank building, now home to Garden's Edge, along Main Street in Hennessey, Oklahoma.

"It's been interesting," Haymaker said of running the store. "The funny part to me is, even in a small town, in a little business in a small town, it's still stressful. I think I'd be stressed no matter what business, but I always have to remind myself that I just live a little ways from where I work, I'm my own boss...I should be relaxed."

Garden's Edge's biggest competitors are big retail stores like Hobby Lobby and Walmart, and the only way to compete with them is to offer better service and more creativity, she said.

Local residents must still go out of town to buy items—say a washer and dryer—that were available in stores along Main Street just a few decades ago. But Hennessey's Main Street has also experienced a bit of resurgence in recent years. A new hotel recently opened, as well as a new store across the street from Garden's Edge.

A few events are held on Main Street, but overall it has been hard to get the business community to come together without a chamber of commerce in place, Haymaker said. "Our individual businesspeople are pretty independent, so it's a little bit hard to get everyone to work together on a big downtown thing."

Though the community has lost some residents over the years, Haymaker said young people are returning with their families for the opportunity to raise their kids in a small-town environment.

"They may not work here. If they're lucky, they'll get a job here, but that may be stretching it. They may commute from a different area like Enid or someplace else, but they like the idea of raising their kid in a smaller school and also where they can go out and play and not get accosted on the street," she said. "I see a lot more kids riding their bicycles around."

Kiowa County

General Tommy Franks Leadership Institute and Museum

507 South Main Street, Hobart

Called "a down-to-earth, no-nonsense" guy by former president George W. Bush and "Pooh" by his grandchildren, General Tommy Franks shows that combining a stern work ethic with a love of family can produce lasting results.

Franks was the United States general who led the wars in Iraq and Afghanistan until his retirement in 2003. Born in Wynnewood, Oklahoma, Franks grew up in Texas, where he graduated from the same high school as the former first lady Laura Bush, whose future husband would describe Franks in such simple—yet positive—terms.

He joined the United States Army in 1965 and, as a second lieutenant, was sent to Vietnam, where he earned six awards for valor and three Purple Hearts. Over the next several decades, Franks would go on to take part in major conflicts all over the world while also completing his undergraduate degree at the University of Texas at Arlington and his master of public administration degree at Shippensburg University in Pennsylvania.

He was promoted to four-star general in June 2000 and tapped to lead the United States Central Command as commander-in-chief. It's there that Franks led the invasions into Afghanistan and Iraq.

Following retirement in 2003, Franks started conducting speeches about leadership and democracy. A few years later, Franks and local community members in Hobart in southwestern Oklahoma developed the General Tommy Franks Leadership Institute and Museum.

The museum "details the history of the military from the Vietnam War to the present," said museum executive director Warren Martin.

A jacket worn by former president George W. Bush in 2001 is among the artifacts and memorabilia on display at the General Tommy Franks Leadership Institute and Museum on Hobart's Main Street.

"And it's really built around the career of General Franks but focuses on all of the military."

The exhibits snake through the building, starting with memorabilia from Franks's childhood such as his first rifle, a replica of his family's living room in Wynnewood and the Franks family Bible. Other noteworthy objects on display include various artifacts from his time serving abroad and a jacket once worn by former president Bush in 2001.

A traveling exhibit room features displays of various themes like 9/11 and Rwanda. "Basically, what we do is we feature any exhibit that really focuses in on the values and the history of southwest Oklahomans—small towns that made General Franks the leader he is—and trying to communicate those values to the world," Martin said.

Visitors to the museum along Main Street are predominantly those with a military background or military history of some sort, Martin said, though some visitors are enthusiasts of Route 66 driving along present-day Interstate 40 who head south trying to get a better understanding of Oklahoma and all that it offers.

What they'll see when they step foot in the museum named in honor of General Franks is part traditional museum and part leadership institute,

Martin said. "One of the unique things they'll find here is that most of our exhibits have a direct tie to leadership principles and leadership values that are found in the life of General Franks and also found in small-town America."

The institute conducts educational programs, seminars and workshops around the state to teach the four principles of leadership: character, communication, common vision and caring.

Franks, who lives with his wife on a ranch in nearby Roosevelt, is chairman of the museum's national board of advisors.

Latimer County

Huskins Guns and Ammo and Camo and Lace

103 East Main Street, Wilburton

Guns and lacy garments. Ammo and accessories. Gun shops and women's boutiques number too many to count in Oklahoma, where the belief in the right to bear arms ranks right up there next to the right to wear comfortable shoes. But a husband-and-wife team in the eastern Oklahoma city of Wilburton has put a spin on the two stores often seen separately on Main Streets: they've opened a combination gun store and women's clothing boutique.

Though composed of two separate stores with two different names, the pistols and semi-automatic rifles at Huskins Guns and Ammo sit just feet away from the dresses and headbands on display at Camo and Lace. Both stores are housed in the historic Huskins building along Wilburton's Main Street that was once home to a pharmacy.

The stores, which opened in March 2013, were the idea of Marnie Boggs-Witt and her husband, Jason Witt, who seem to have been destined to get married: the couple's grandparents were friends growing up in Wilburton, and their parents went to school together, too. Boggs-Witt's aunt, in fact, babysat for her future husband when he was a child.

"We were going to originally just do the gun store, and I wanted to bring in some stuff to get women in there," said Marnie Boggs-Witt.

Soon, though, the couple realized that there wasn't really a boutique-type store along Main Street in the city of 2,840 inhabitants, so they decided to go ahead and open Camo and Lace along with Huskins Guns.

Camo and Lace features ATX Mafia clothing, leggings, tunics and other clothing as well as jewelry and other accessories. Boggs-Witt also stocks

University of Oklahoma and Oklahoma State University apparel and some hunting gear for women. Huskins Guns is stocked with guns, gun accessories and ammunition.

The combination store has worked well in attracting shoppers who may have not otherwise planned on purchasing anything. "A lot of women will come in with the guys and not realize there is other stuff. And a lot of guys will come in with women and not realize the guns are there," said Boggs-Witt.

Each of the stores has its own website and Facebook page for customers to learn about merchandise, and the couple also advertises in the local newspaper. The old adage that you have to spend money to make money is true when it came to opening up the combined stores, Boggs-Witt said, noting that at least at first, any profit made is spent bringing in new products and paying bills. "That's probably why a lot of people aren't willing to go into business for themselves," the forty-year-old said. "The first couple of years you're pretty much broke."

Still, the two, who also own a photography business, were determined to work for themselves, no matter how difficult. "You have to decide to do it until you just can't do it anymore or until it goes big. We're hoping it goes big," Boggs-Witt said.

Le Flore County

True Grit Day

Main Street, Spiro

True Grit, the 1968 novel that transported readers back to the Wild West days of the 1800s and was later adapted into a movie, came to life along Main Street in tiny Spiro, located in eastern Oklahoma, where many of the scenes in the original novel were set.

In the novel by Charles Portis, Mattie Ross recounts how she avenged the death of her father, Frank Ross, after he was killed by Tom Chaney.

Capitalizing on its ties to the book, the Spiro Public Library held the first-ever True Grit Day with a reenactment of the main characters' gunfight, a character look-alike contest, stick-horse races and horse-and-buggy rides.

Participants were also invited to eat like they did back in the 1800s, including a chuck wagon feed with beans and corn bread. The event was held in conjunction with the annual Spiro Car Show and Craft Show.

Glenda Stokes, Spiro librarian and president of the board of directors for the Spiro Chamber of Commerce, said the event was put on thanks to a grant from the National Endowment for the Humanities in conjunction with Arts Midwest.

The library, Stokes said, is the hub of the community in Spiro, population 2,160. In addition to providing the basics of a library—books and magazines to check out and help with research projects, for example—it also provides for individual community members. At Christmastime, an Angel Tree is set up to provide all kids in the community with presents, while an Easter egg hunt offers fun and excitement in the spring. Those devastated by a fire or another natural disaster can also turn to the library, which offers household items and clothes for people who have been displaced.

Lincoln County

Rock Café

114 West Main Street, Stroud

I didn't know anything about Route 66 or how to cook. There were so many things I didn't know.
—Dawn Welch, owner of the Rock Café and inspiration for the character Sally in the Disney film Cars

Tourists journeying along Route 66 in Oklahoma have been stopping at the Rock Café on Stroud's Main Street for more than seventy years, but it's only been in the past two decades that the restaurant has become a cultural icon for the famed highway's resurgence and its owner an inspiration for the character Sally in the Pixar animated film *Cars*.

Dawn Welch never thought she would end up in Stroud, a city of about 2,700 people located in eastern Lincoln County. Welch, who grew up seventy miles away in Yukon, was working for a cruise line and was planning to head to Costa Rica and open up a café when she returned to Oklahoma with plans to sell some property she'd recently inherited.

No sooner did she arrive than she learned about the café, a sandstone building that was built in the 1930s by Roy Rives. Shut down for several years before Welch's arrival, the café had become a symbol of Route 66's decay. "It had a very bad reputation, and everybody in town told me there was no way I could possibly rebuild that reputation," she said.

But Welch decided to give it a try. At age twenty-four, she decided to reopen the restaurant, initially for one year. She rented the building for $200 per month from the previous owner and went about learning all she could

Route 66 enthusiasts flock to the Rock Café along Main Street in Stroud, Oklahoma.

about the community—a tip she learned in a book she purchased about running a restaurant.

She may have known very little about operating a restaurant, how to cook or Route 66 history, but she knew all she had to do to keep afloat was sell ten hamburgers, Cokes and orders of french fries per day.

When the restaurant reopened in February 1993, Welch did that and much more. By March, international visitors began arriving at her doorstep. One group from Belgium started talking about Route 66, Welch said. "And I was like, 'Where is that?'" she said. "And they started laughing at me. And that's when I realized I was still in the tourism business."

Welch soon began feeling at home. Route 66 became her ocean and the Rock Café her ship. She decided to stay in Stroud and focus on the café and become its owner.

"It's a daily struggle in a small business, especially in a small town in a small business to make it through the week," she said. "You're always chasing the dream."

In the early 2000s, Welch was chasing that dream—trying to get some money from the National Park Service to help update some of the outdated utilities and equipment in her café—when director John Lasseter and Michael Wallis, a Route 66 historian and author, met up with her. The two were traveling along the highway researching an upcoming animated film about Route 66.

Watching *Cars*, it's easy to see the similarities between Welch and Sally, a Porsche and lawyer who decides to settle down in a cozy community and open up a refurbished motel. Welch was the inspiration. "I had agreed to do this because as a kid I loved Walt Disney," the forty-four-year-old Welch said. "And I thought, 'I always watch *Snow White*.' I thought if Route 66 can be a part of a Disney movie, I knew the longevity of that never dies. We all show *Snow White* still. I knew that it would be a legacy that went on forever."

Even before the film was released, business at the restaurant spiked, and Welch started seeing American tourists once again driving the highway that had been mostly populated by Europeans eager to trace the path and learn about the changing landscapes and cultures of America.

Just a few short years after the film's release, the café was nearly lost as a result of a fire that destroyed the building's roof and much of the interior. Despite the loss, Welch decided to rebuild with the help of family and friends and documented her quest online.

Now, the restaurant is better than ever. About 150 to 200 people a day stop at the Rock Café, its large neon sign out front and the gift shop next door. The café, which was listed on the National Register of Historic Places in 2001, is only open for breakfast and lunch and serves omelets, salads, sandwiches, hot dogs, crepes and more.

The café and Route 66 have helped keep Stroud's Main Street alive, Welch said. "Route 66 has saved our Main Street, for sure. It's made 50 percent of our buildings a viable concept."

Logan County

Lucille's Restaurant

Main Street, Mulhall

Everywhere in this tiny town, the Mulhall name rules supreme. Originally named Alfred, the town was changed to Mulhall in honor of Zachary Mulhall, a ranch owner who became mayor in 1890. In 1900, the town reached its peak population with just over 560 residents.

It was around this time that Zachary Mulhall's Wild West show gained steam. Mulhall's show, though, had something that the many other similarly themed shows lacked—his daughter Lucille. Born in 1885 in St. Louis, Lucille spent her childhood learning to rope, ride, lasso and shoot on the eighty thousand acres that made up the Mulhall Ranch, and she became known as "America's First Cowgirl."

Among the many spectators she impressed as the headliner of her father's show was Teddy Roosevelt, who campaigned in Oklahoma Territory in 1900 and watched in awe as a young Lucille showed off her skills.

Lucille continued to travel and perform her tricks for audiences until she was killed in a car accident at age fifty-five. In 1975, she was posthumously inducted into the National Rodeo Hall of Fame.

Today, large black-and-white photographs of the young cowgirl along with faded newspaper clippings about the Wild West show hang inside the restaurant bearing her name along Main Street in Mulhall.

The population of the central Oklahoma town fifty miles north of Oklahoma City has dwindled over the years—latest census figures peg it at 225—but the legacies of Lucille and her father live on at the restaurant.

Lucille's Restaurant has been in the path of destruction a few times. In 1999, much of Mulhall was destroyed when a violent F-4 tornado barreled

Above: The old Lucille's Restaurant and Bar in Mulhall, Oklahoma.

Left: The current Lucille's in Mulhall, Oklahoma.

through town, though Lucille's was spared. The restaurant wasn't so lucky in 2009, though, when lightning and a subsequent fire caused major damage to the restaurant. At that point, Lucille's was located in the former Oklahoma State Bank Building, a historic two-story, red brick building with expansive windows. Two years later, Lucille's relocated and reopened in a new building across the street, adding a new outdoor patio with wooden rocking chairs and plenty of seating.

Inside, animal skins hang on the wall along with a Choctaw war bonnet that reminds people of the origins of Oklahoma's name. In Choctaw, *okla* means red while *humma* means people.

In addition to describing the food choices available—a variety of steaks, salads and fried chicken dishes—the menu recounts Lucille's life story of hard work, fame and legacy.

The menu ends with this paragraph:

> *Though we've made her seem glamorous, Lucille was the real deal. A hard working, earnest cowgirl, she came by her talents honestly by learning them day in and day out on the ranch. She was tough and determined. Characteristics that we still admire today and wish we saw more of.*

Love County

Photographs by Lawrence

311 West Main Street, Marietta

Lawrence Anderson has been photographing weddings, high school seniors, babies and many other events for nearly thirty years, but there's still one question he has a hard time answering: what made him interested in photography?

Photographs by Lawrence along Main Street in Marietta, Oklahoma.

Caesar's Barber Shop and Bail Bonds in Marietta, Oklahoma.

"That's the question of the day. I have no earthly idea how to answer that question, and I'm asked that every day," he said.

Though not the only photographer in the south-central Oklahoma city of 2,600—"Everybody is doing it now. You got a camera, you're a photographer now," Anderson said—he's the only one with a physical building for an office, located right along Marietta's Main Street, which he said he chose for its visibility.

His building, which has a prominent sign out front with a camera and the name of his business, is just down the street from one of the community's most offbeat businesses, a combination barbershop and bail bondsman.

Owned by Marietta mayor James Lang, Caesar's Barber Shop and Bail Bonds is the only place in town where someone can get their hair cut and obtain money to get out of jail all in one place.

Marietta is the county seat of Love County, and the county courthouse is also located on Main Street. Dedicated in 1910, it was the first county courthouse built after Oklahoma became a state in 1907 and was listed on the National Register of Historic Places in 1984.

Over the years, the city of Marietta has suffered a bit with the advent of Interstate 35 on the edge of town, eliminating the need for travelers to drive through the community and possibly purchase an item at one of the Main Street stores.

Major County

Jensen's

218 South Main Street, Fairview

This is an icon to Fairview. People associate Fairview with it.
—Todd Smith

Historic signs can tell you a lot about a place. Cracked paint, blown-out light bulbs and rusty features are all clues that a community didn't care enough—or, in some cases, didn't have enough money—to preserve the vintage signs and advertising that once dotted the landscape.

Well-lit, freshly painted signs show that someone took the time necessary to restore a sign to its original glory.

In Fairview, restoring the namesake sign that hangs from the Jensen's building has never been necessary. For more than fifty years, it's been a landmark all its own in this northwestern Oklahoma city of 2,600.

"Call it a time capsule," said Smith, a third-generation car dealer. "It's really something special."

But for the residents of Fairview, there's been something noticeably absent from the building for the past few years. A large eagle statue weighing hundreds of pounds once sat on the corner of the roof, standing watch over the community. The statue, which had been around for several decades, was a symbol of the Case tractor company. Then one day a few years ago, the bulky statue mysteriously disappeared from its perch atop the roof, never to be found again.

Jensen's, however, continues to thrive. Started by Alfred Jensen in 1931, it moved into the current building on Main Street in the 1950s, Smith said.

Jensen's is a third-generation company in Fairview, Oklahoma.

It's recognized as the oldest continually operated GMC dealer in Oklahoma. Smith's wife, Sue, is Alfred Jensen's granddaughter.

Though the Jensen family has sold everything from guns to boats over the years, the dealership mainly focuses on cars and tractors now.

"To be here for eighty-plus years, you have to be doing something right," Smith said.

The third-generation dealer believes the business's success goes back to something simple: relationships.

"A small-town dealer is unique in a lot of ways. We deal more with relationships and value relationships," he said. "In a small community, if we do somebody wrong, everyone would know about it."

Marshall County

National Sand Bass Festival

Main Street, Madill

Though the National Sand Bass Festival may celebrate the freshwater fish and its impact on this south-central Oklahoma city, don't look for many of the creatures during the weeklong event.

Music—and lots of it—has replaced the original fish tournament and fish fry that brought in thousands of people in years past. But the change of focus from the wriggling creatures to down-home country music is reeling in a new generation of festival-goers.

The festival was originally started in 1963 as a way for local businessmen to show their appreciation to the many visitors who came through the area during the summer months, said Donny Raley, who has been involved with the festival since he was a kid and is now chairman of the committee that organizes it. Recognizing that tourism was the Madill area's biggest industry because of nearby Lake Texoma, the businessmen hoped to capitalize on that with the festival, which featured a large fishing tournament. All the fish caught during the week were cooked up and served free of charge to festival-goers during a large fish fry.

The fishing, food and fun attracted larger and larger numbers of visitors each year. It soon grew too big, too fast, though.

Local law enforcement was overwhelmed with security at the 1974 festival, when more than twenty-seven thousand plates of fish were served to people, and the governor of Oklahoma sent in the Army National Guard to help with the crowds, Raley said.

Organizers of the festival decided to shut it down the following year, and the festival was discontinued for several years until 1987, when a new generation decided to bring it back.

This time, however, the festival's signature fishing tournament and fish fry were replaced with Nashville-worthy entertainment. (A fishing tournament for kids still takes place.) "It has been a huge success so far," Raley said of the new festival lineup.

Although organizers don't count how many people come to the festival, which is held in Madill's Courthouse Square on Main Street, Raley and others estimate that tens of thousands of people descend on the city of about 3,800 during the festival's six-day run.

For the local merchants in and around Main Street and the rest of Madill, the festival, always held during the first full week of June, offers an opportunity to attract new customers through special sales and promotions. "One business owner describes this week as equal to a Christmas shopping week for him," Raley said.

Mayes County

Main Street, Spavinaw

Hall of Fame baseball player Mickey Mantle is Spavinaw's most famous local to make it to the big time. Though Mantle grew up in Commerce, about forty-five miles north, Spavinaw is where he was born on October 20, 1931. The town of about 430 people in northeastern Mayes County takes pride in its connection to the famous ballplayer, who was considered the greatest switch-hitter of all time. It's evident in the black-and-white portrait of the player on an abandoned storefront window along the town's Main Street. Wearing his signature Yankees uniform and a pensive look on his face, the portrait depicts Mantle at the height of his famed career when he helped lead the New York Yankees to seven World Championships.

Discovered as a teenager playing for a team in Kansas, Mantle signed his professional contract on the same day he graduated high school. The $140-a-month salary plus a signing bonus of more than $1,100 must have seemed like a dream come true for the young player in 1948. He played eighteen seasons with the Yankees and holds the record for most World Series home runs. He died in 1995.

In 2004, a stretch of State Highway 82/20 was renamed in his honor. Two years later, on what would have been Mantle's seventy-fifth birthday, the community of Spavinaw came together to celebrate the wunderkind.

The portrait paying homage to the community's most famous son on an abandoned, neglected building is emblematic of much of Spavinaw's Main Street.

Main Street in Spavinaw, Oklahoma.

Spavinaw's most famous resident, Mickey Mantle, is memorialized on a building along Main Street.

While Main Street seemed to be a thriving area of commerce at one point, many of the buildings along the street now look as if they were deserted in a hurry.

Advertised as having a complete music store, restaurant, bait and tackle and grocery store, the Copperhead Mall still has signs and decorations hanging outside despite the building becoming overrun with weeds.

Despite the dying commercial district, residents like Jodi Read say they are proud to call Spavinaw home.

"We love this country—all the lakes and there's nice people in this town," Read said as she sat on her front porch stringing fishing line.

McClain County

Hotel Love

200 West Main Street, Purcell

Back in the late 1800s and early 1900s, visitors to the Chickasaw Nation had luxury at their fingertips. For two dollars a night, visitors to the area could relax at the Hotel Love with a variety of amenities including steam heat and electric lights.

Built in 1895, the sixty-three-room Hotel Love was considered the pride of Purcell and one of the grandest hotels in all of the Chickasaw Nation. It was named for Jeremiah Love, a rancher from Missouri who moved to Indian Territory in hopes of a better life.

Hotel Love, now known as Butler's Antiques, in Purcell, Oklahoma.

Once settled in his new home, he met and married Sallie Gaines Criner, a Chickasaw tribal member, with whom he had ten children. Jeremiah Love became a well-known businessman in the community, creating the Chickasaw National Bank, where he served as president, and the Hotel Love.

Nearly a century after its opening, Jerry and Elaine Butler opened Butler's Antiques inside the former Hotel Love. More than a dozen rooms in the historic building are filled with collectibles, photographs, books, glassware and other antique items.

Running the antique business is enjoyable, Jerry Butler said, and having it located in the building once known as the Hotel Love is an added bonus. Main Street businesses, he said, are the heart of a small town.

McCurtain County

Wooden Animal Statues

Main Street, Broken Bow

The timber industry is big business in this southeastern Oklahoma city that's just minutes from Beavers Bend State Park, so it's little wonder that city leaders turned to their most abundant resource in order to spice up the downtown commercial district along Main Street.

Wooden sculptures line Main Street in Broken Bow, Oklahoma.

Wooden carved statues of beavers, bears, a deer and other animals sit in the flower beds lining the street, a tribute to the wildlife native to the Kiamichi Mountains region.

"People love them," said Broken Bow city clerk Amanda Eccles. "They're very unique. You don't see them in every town across the nation."

Leaders in the city of 4,120 residents purchased the first batch of statues back in 2011 from a couple in nearby Valliant who created them. The placement of the statues coincided with new landscaping along Main Street.

Though the carvings are much smaller than the real-life versions of the animals, visitors to Main Street will be amazed with the detail involved. A brown bear wraps his paws around a tree in one sculpture, while a wolf howls at the moon in another.

In front of the Broken Bow Police Department on Main Street sits a wood carving of a police badge.

"Most everything we carved is kind of important to this area," Eccles said.

McIntosh County

Our Favorite Place

127 North Main Street, Eufaula

Oklahoma may be known for twisters, churches and rednecks, but Karen Weldin thinks it should be known for something else: the artists, musicians and home-grown entrepreneurs who are eager to show off their creativity.

That's why Weldin has opened up Our Favorite Place, an art gallery and store featuring only products made by Oklahomans. The locally made products for sale include honey, jams, jellies, pretzels, chocolate, T-shirts and even soap. Coffee roasted in Mustang is sold at a coffee shop inside the store, and people can spend hours perusing the books by Oklahoma authors or surfing the web using the free Wi-Fi.

"The creativity in Oklahoma is unbelievable," Weldin said, listing off all the types of innovative people she works with including artists, musicians and authors. "We need to be supporting them."

And support them she has. Weldin, a self-proclaimed lake person, moved to Eufaula from Oklahoma City to be closer to her beloved Lake Eufaula. Once she did, she got into real estate and bought a historic building on Main Street that she fell in love with upon learning its one-hundred-year-old history. She decided to forgo leasing it out as originally planned, instead turning it into Our Favorite Place.

"I tell people I made the worst real estate mistake a realtor can make. I said I got emotionally attached to the building. I fell in love with the building and decided I wanted to hang on to it and do something with it," Weldin said of the building that was at varying times a bakery and shoe store.

That something became Our Favorite Place. With more than one hundred artists and vendors from Oklahoma selling their work, shoppers are bound to find what they are looking for. Some of the artists are also sharing their skills through classes at the store. Initially, Weldin, age sixty, sought out the artists and vendors, but she doesn't have to worry about that anymore. "I was hunting them, but about six months after we opened, I didn't have to do that anymore. People were hearing about Our Favorite Place, and now they contact me and ask to be in the store."

A selection committee decides who makes the cut based on an application and photographs of the artwork and products, she said.

"I think it's so important for us to support jobs and the small-business person, not just in Oklahoma, but in the United States."

Murray County

Arbuckle Historical Museum

12 Main Street, Davis

The Arbuckle Historical Museum is brimming with history, and it's not just inside the yellow building with the red roof. The building itself, the former depot for the Atchison, Topeka and Santa Fe Railway, was instrumental in the formation of the city of Davis, located in south-central Oklahoma.

Constructed in 1908, the one-story depot served freight and passenger lines as they traversed the rail's twelve thousand miles of track between Chicago and San Francisco and south to Galveston, Texas.

Like other depots and establishments across the South, white passengers and black passengers were segregated. There were two separate waiting areas depending on the color of the passenger's skin. White passengers arriving at the depot entered their expansive waiting room from the front of the depot. Black passengers, meanwhile, entered their more cramped waiting area—which also housed luggage—from the back.

A separate ticket counter for black passengers was later encased.

The building, which serves as a sort of marker to the entrance of Davis's downtown commercial district, now houses the Arbuckle Historical Museum of Davis. Named for the ancient Arbuckle Mountains nearby, the museum features pictures, artifacts, school displays and a printing press, among other items, for people to see a slice of Davis's history. One room highlights frontier life, taking visitors back to territorial days.

Muskogee County

Erly Rush Coffeehouse

200 South Main Street, Muskogee

Nick Wilks had always dreamed of owning and operating his own coffee shop, so when the opportunity came about for him to return to his roots in Muskogee and share his love of java, he jumped at the chance.

In the fall of 2012, Wilks, twenty-four, opened up Erly Rush Coffeehouse along Main Street in Muskogee, a city of 39,000 and the county seat, after winning a competition put on by the local downtown revitalization organization, Downtown Muskogee Inc. The competition pitted prospective business owners against each other to come up with the best blueprint for opening a new store, restaurant or other outlet in downtown Muskogee.

Erly Rush Coffeehouse (named in honor of his grandmother whom he used to call Erly and not a play on the hustle and bustle of the morning) and Wilks won $5,000 to help with advertising, marketing and designing from Downtown Muskogee Inc.—along with bragging rights. Now, the aroma of a variety of coffees wafts through the air as visitors enter the store.

"It's always a lot of work," Wilks said of the store.

In addition to Erly Rush, Wilks and his mother bought five other buildings to turn into antiques stores. In fact, Wilks and his mother, Sherry, own Hattie's House Antiques next door to Erly Rush.

"It was just a godsend thing," Nick Wilks said.

Noble County

The Rock

Main Street, Red Rock

As pastor of Otoe Baptist Church in Red Rock, Jimmy Kenner wears many hats: he's confidant and adviser to his many parishioners; he's a driver for those needing help getting to a doctor's appointment or to a new job; he's a fundraiser for the poor and less fortunate; and he's a cook for the hungry.

Kenner moved to Oklahoma, specifically to the town of Red Rock, in 2004 from Kentucky with his wife after he heard some of the churches catering to Native American worshipers were looking for pastors.

In 2006, the couple opened up the Rock in a former city hall building along Red Rock's sparse Main Street to provide a variety of needs for community members in and around Red Rock, which is home to the headquarters of the Otoe-Missouria Tribe. It's where people can buy cheap food from the grill that Kenner, his wife and another worker cook. It's also where residents turn for clothes, household items and ministry and guidance from Kenner.

"There was nothing for them to do" before the Rock opened, Kenner said of the town's fewer than three hundred residents. The Rock has become a sort of community-gathering spot for citizens.

The Rock is an offshoot of the Otoe Baptist Ministry and is where people—both church members and nonmembers—go to sit down, talk to each other and eat.

"We've seen people come together from all walks, which is pretty great," Kenner said.

Kenner, his wife and another staff member grill food to sell to ranchers and others who stop in during the week, and the money raised helps cover

The Rock community center in Red Rock, Oklahoma.

the cost for other items at the church, located just a few blocks away from the Rock, he said.

"It started out we didn't know what we were doing," Kenner said, laughing. He and his wife started out with a tiny grill, but the Otoe-Missouria Tribe donated a larger grill and other cooking utensils and accessories.

"People work together," he said. "We don't have a lot of resources, but together we do."

Although Red Rock is a small, rural community, it's home to two Baptist churches: the Kenner-led Otoe Baptist Church, which has about fifty parishioners a week who are primarily Native American, and the First Baptist Church, which has a mostly white congregation, Kenner said.

The Otoe-Missouria Tribe has a large presence in Red Rock. Composed of nearly three thousand tribal members—the majority of whom live in Oklahoma—the Otoes and Missourians originated in the Great Lakes Region near present-day Michigan before migrating to Missouri.

The Otoe-Missouria Tribe was relocated to Red Rock in 1881. Like a lot of other Native American tribes, their language has been lost over time, and the Otoe-Missourians are working to preserve and revitalize it for future generations. Financial ventures for the tribe include convenience stores, casinos, a hotel and a cattle ranch.

At one point, the tribe owned a farm cooperative at the end of Red Rock's Main Street.

Other businesses along Red Rock's Main Street include a mechanic and a pecan business, where residents bring their pecans to be shelled starting in late October through the early spring.

"We're just a small, little rural community," Kenner said. "We enjoy living here and have met a lot of nice people."

Nowata County

Phyllis Pryor

Main Street, Delaware

It's just a typical small town anymore, and like I said, they're all dying out. And it's sad. The people in small towns were really the backbone of the country at one time, along with the farmers.
—Phyllis Pryor

Seventy-eight-year-old Phyllis Pryor can only imagine what Main Street in Delaware, located in Nowata County in northeast Oklahoma, used to look like decades ago: a streetcar picked up and dropped off passengers as they scurried from the hotel to the bank to the store and back.

Now, though, Pryor looks out as she stands outside her one-story home on Main Street and sees homes—some mobile—that are in desperate need of cleanup and repair.

She doesn't hold any hope that Delaware, population of a little more than four hundred citizens, will ever return to its heyday of the early 1900s, when four thousand people called the town home after oil was found nearby. But she just hopes it cleans up. "Some of the people are starting to keep their yards up a bit better. But what do you do? They have an ordinance, but they don't enforce it," she said.

Growing up out in the country in nearby Childers, Pryor remembers riding her horse and exploring unknown areas, never worrying about her safety. Kids growing up today don't have the same opportunity for that, she

Phyllis Pryor stands outside her home along Main Street in Delaware, Oklahoma.

Chickens roam a lot at the intersection of Cherokee and Main Streets in Delaware, Oklahoma.

said. "We had that freedom and lack of fear. We never locked our doors, never thought about it," she said.

She moved to Delaware in 1951 and graduated a few years later from the local high school, just down the road from where she currently resides. The school has burned down, and now students go to Oklahoma Union, about ten miles north in South Coffeyville. After living out of state for years, Pryor decided to move back in 2003 after her husband retired to be closer to other family members. Her husband has since passed away.

When Pryor moved back, she said she noticed that most of the homeowners had long since left, leaving their property to tenants who didn't seem to have the same pride in keeping up with it and left it to deteriorate.

There's now only one grocery store in town, located along Cherokee Street, which has become the main thoroughfare through the community. At the intersection of Cherokee and Main Streets, chickens and a cow are enclosed in a fenced-in lot and watch as motorists drive by.

Aside from the grocery store, the only other establishment in town is the post office, where Pryor works. Named for the Eastern Delaware tribe whose members migrated from Kansas, the town of Delaware had its first post office established on March 19, 1898. The town quickly ballooned to several thousand inhabitants and several businesses following the discovery of oil, but the lightning-fast population growth was unsustainable, and the population dipped to its lowest level of just more than one hundred by 1907. It has resurged since then but still struggles to keep residents. The post office, in fact, is managed remotely, operating under the postmaster in Nowata, located about six miles away. And recently, the Delaware post office cut down from eight-hour days to four-hour days, despite a steady stream of customers, Pryor said, adding that she believes it's only a matter of time before all small-town post offices are shut down permanently.

Okfuskee County

Main Street, Clearview

A few houses (one with a front porch overflowing with knickknacks, or trash, depending on how you look at it) and buildings (one advertising live bait) line Clearview's Main Street, reminders of what once was in this all-black town located in east-central Oklahoma that thrived during the early 1900s but now has only about fifty residents. Many of those buildings and homes now sit empty and abandoned.

"Ain't nothing open on Main Street. Ain't nothing. Everything's closed down. There ain't nothing," one longtime resident said as he stood outside his friend's home on a dreary, rain-soaked day.

Clearview is one of thirteen all-black towns still remaining in Oklahoma. In the latter half of the 1800s and into the early 1900s, slaves belonging to Native American tribes migrated with their owners and former owners to what is present-day Oklahoma. The slaves were allowed to live away from their owners or Indian families in small communities that later developed into larger communities named after prominent family members. As many as seventy towns and communities sprang up as promoters in the South advertised the new all-black settlements, said historian Shirley Nero, who grew up in and currently lives in Clearview. Nero leads a tour of all-black towns in Oklahoma for people wanting to learn more about the settlements.

The advertisements—very elaborate and descriptive of the area—appeared in newspapers and were shared through traveling preachers, family members and other means, Nero said. They highlighted what the land and

An abandoned building on Main Street in Clearview, Oklahoma.

Main Street in Clearview, Oklahoma.

An abandoned building along Main Street in Clearview, Oklahoma.

communities could offer: plenty of acres and water to farm, schools for children and, most importantly, freedom.

"The people could be free to do what they wanted, to start a new beginning, to govern themselves without the control of someone else," Nero added. Many of the all-black towns sprang up near Native American communities, and both African American people and Native American people worked side by side. In fact, many of the black people had Native American heritage.

The all-black towns began to die out in the 1920s and 1930s as the Great Depression hit, forcing residents to move elsewhere for work, and railroads left town, leaving residents immobile. The schools closed in the 1960s, Nero said.

Although only a few still exist today, all-black towns are an important part of Oklahoma's history, Nero said, because they represent people who once struggled from oppression but came to Oklahoma for a fresh start with their families in search of freedom of education, religion, prejudice and life itself.

Tours of some of the black towns have brought renewed attention to their unique place in Oklahoma's history. Nero said she hopes that people realize each surviving town has a rich history that needs to be preserved and promoted.

"We need ideas and contributions to help keep the towns alive," she said. "Each year, there are fewer and fewer of us. We need money and we need people to move into the towns. We must not die out."

Oklahoma County

Former Tuton's Drugstore Building

Corner of First and Main Streets, Arcadia

Aficionados of Route 66 history and lore are big fans of the diminutive town of Arcadia—population 250—located just twenty-five miles northeast of downtown Oklahoma City. The bedroom community boasts two of the most popular icons in Oklahoma: a restored round, red barn simply known as the Arcadia Round Barn and POPS, a modern restaurant boasting a multitude of soda flavors and a sixty-six-foot-tall soda-bottle-with-straw sculpture.

Just off Route 66, however, along Arcadia's quaint Main Street, travelers can find another historical gem. Situated at the corner of First and Main Streets, the two-story sandstone building known most for its time as a drugstore features arched doorways and windows.

The First State Bank of Arcadia constructed the building in 1917 by cutting sandstone from a nearby farm and hauling it to the building site. The bank moved in but only remained for a few years before it was sold to the enterprising duo of George Blake and Benjamin Franklin Tuton, who by that time had been running a successful pharmacy nearby for several years.

As the drugstore continued to prosper, thanks in part to sales from its popular soda fountain and ice cream, one of Tuton's two sons soon got into the business while Blake was bought out. But in June 1924, a fire ravaged Arcadia's business community, and the only building to withstand the blaze was the drugstore.

The damage from the fire coupled with the effects of urbanization started to cause problems for the small town, and the store closed in 1941. The

Tuton's Drugstore in Arcadia is listed on the National Register of Historic Places.

building, however, remained in the family. It was leased out in 1945 and reopened as a grocery store. Tuton's granddaughter preserved the store's original fountain, furniture and cash register, hoping that it would one day be used when Tuton's reopened.

Sadly, that hasn't happened. Over the years, a combination art gallery and real estate business opened in the building, which is listed on the National Register of Historic Places, and it now houses a photography business.

Okmulgee County

Readings by Jaycee

208 East Main Street, Henryetta

A strange feeling overcame Jaycee Marks as she was driving from her home in Baton Rouge, Louisiana, to Tulsa in January 2013. It was a feeling, she said, that she has felt many times in her thirty-seven years of life: a spirit was guiding her.

This time, God was telling her to take the exit for Henryetta, a city of six thousand in Okmulgee County in east-central Oklahoma. At 10:30 p.m., Marks, who calls herself a psychic, obliged and ended up on Main Street. Once there, she located a small house that now doubles as her office and found a new home for her and her family.

"We just turned on to Main Street off of the turnpike and I said, 'This looks exactly like my vision.' And sure enough, it was right here," she said.

There are people in Henryetta and the surrounding area who need guidance, Marks believes, and she is in town to offer her help. She noted that there is no other psychic in Henryetta, though there are readers in Tulsa and Oklahoma City.

"Everybody is intrigued by the future. Everybody wants to know what is held for them in the future," said Marks, who conducts palm readings, tarot card readings, psychic readings, spiritual readings and crystal readings. As a psychic, Marks said, she doesn't sugarcoat any of the visions she sees. If someone walks through her door, they obviously want to know about the future—good or bad.

"If I see you're going to die, then I'm going to tell you you're going to die. If I see there is some kind of bad accident that is going to happen to you,

Readings by Jaycee in Henryetta, Oklahoma.

well, I'm going to tell you that. I don't hold nothing back," said Marks, who also does readings in Virginia and Louisiana.

Marks said she first discovered her ability to see the future and read people's fortunes as a three-year-old who was near death. God came to her, she said, and told her she was meant to help people and he was going to bless her with this gift for seeing the future and helping people through problems in their lives.

"Ever since then I've had this gift that I can just read people—a spiritual reading, palm reading and help them, guide them, bring them back to God," she said. "Through God there is nothing that is impossible, and there are a lot of people around here that lost faith and needs to get closer to the Lord."

But don't expect Marks to know whether or not her husband is going to get that big raise or if her son will hit the jackpot someday; she can't see or read the future of any of her family members, she said.

Initially, Marks and her family met some resistance when they moved to Henryetta, but that has dissipated, and she calls the community "awesome."

"There are a lot of people that wasn't very welcoming from the beginning, but now that they see I'm not a witch or do voodoo or black magic and I only work through God's spirit, I've been accepted a lot better," she said. "It just took time for people to see what I was about and that I wasn't a fly-by-night, here today, gone tomorrow—that I'm trying to make Henryetta my home for my family, for my kids."

Curious clients—often as many as three a day—quickly arrived at the new business once it opened in hopes of knowing their future. But as time passed, the numbers have slowed down to a trickle, and now Marks sees one or two people a week, mostly return customers. Still, she remains hopeful for the future of her business and her new hometown.

"As long as God permits me to be here, I will be here. For as long as it takes."

Osage County

Bigheart Museum

616 West Main Street, Barnsdall

Anyone who passes through this community in Osage County may be a bit confused by what to call it. Though the city of 1,200 has officially gone by the name of Barnsdall for more than a century, another name is all over the community's Main Street. The town's historical museum is called the Bigheart Museum. The annual festival celebrating the community is also known as Bigheart, and signs lining the street call it that.

"It's kind of a touchy subject. It was really illegally changed," Joe Williams, president of the Bigheart Museum, said as he sat in the small white building commemorating the town's history.

The community was originally named for Chief James Bigheart, a member of the Osage Indian tribe who moved to Indian Territory in 1872. After becoming chief in 1875, one of many acts Bigheart did for the tribe was to sign an oil lease on behalf of the Osage people that helped them to become the wealthiest tribe in America during the 1920s. Tribal members became so wealthy, in fact, that some were killed. Known as the Osage "Reign of Terror," an estimated twenty-four Osage tribal members died under suspicious circumstances in the 1920s in Osage County, and it's believed that many of the tribal members were killed for their headrights, shares of the tribe's oil royalties.

On March 3, 1905, the community was formed and named in honor of James Bigheart. Less than twenty years later, a petition was filed to change the name for another well-known local whose last name started with the second letter of the alphabet. After two-thirds of the people voted for the change,

This old typewriter is one of many items on display at the Bigheart Museum in Barnsdall, Oklahoma.

The exterior of the Bigheart Museum in Barnsdall, Oklahoma.

Bigheart was renamed Barnsdall on January 1, 1922, to honor Theodore N. Barnsdall, an oil tycoon from Pennsylvania who came to Oklahoma to acquire and expand a local oil refinery company. Both Bigheart and Barnsdall had died by the time the community changed names.

Today, pictures of the two men hang near each other at the Bigheart Museum along Barnsdall's Main Street. The museum is a hodgepodge of history and includes old photos, newspaper articles, yearbooks, medicine bottles, dolls and more.

"We keep the history of Barnsdall and Bigheart," said Williams, who has been president of the museum since 1999. The museum is open by appointment only, Williams said, a consequence of a lack of interest and a lack of money.

"We used to see six to ten [people] a day," he said. "Now we don't see anyone anymore unless we open for them. There's nothing in town anymore."

In the 1910s, Bigheart saw a trio of natural disasters. A tornado tore through town on April 12, 1911, destroying several homes and barns. The following year, a fire broke out that destroyed about half of the town's businesses, causing about $50,000 in damages. And in 1915, nearby water from Bird Creek flooded the eastern half of the city, damaging several bridges.

When oil exploration was at its peak in the area in the 1920s, Barnsdall's population boomed to 2,000 people. Now it has about 1,200.

"It's kind of like the gold rush," Williams said. "While everyone came in for the gold rush, that's like Barnsdall with oil. Everyone came, but they've all left."

An oil well built in 1914 sits in the middle of Main Street. Listed on the National Register of Historic Places in 1997, it's a constant reminder of the role oil played in this small northeastern Oklahoma community. The annual Bigheart Day is held each year during Memorial Day weekend along Main Street and features arts and crafts, food vendors, a parade and more.

Ottawa County

Coleman Theatre

103 North Main Street, Miami

Like a handful of other Main Streets in Oklahoma, the celebrated Route 66 plays an important role in the history, development and resurgence of Miami's main avenue through town.

Miami boasts the longest Main Street along Route 66 in Oklahoma, and the historical highway has had a significant impact on the revitalization of the downtown community, which was listed on the National Register of Historic Places in 2009. The city of 13,570 is less than twenty miles from both Kansas and Missouri.

Main Street is home to several notable Route 66 attractions, including the Route 66 Vintage Iron Motorcycle Museum, which features more than twenty-five vintage motorcycles and exhibits; Waylan's Ku-Ku Burger, a classic restaurant from the 1960s with cooked-to-order food; and the Miami Marathon Oil Company Service Station, built in 1929 and believed to be the oldest standing Marathon Oil Station.

Vintage signs lining Main Street and several stores with Route 66 memorabilia also add to the nostalgia. As drivers travel north along Main Street and enter Miami's downtown area, they are greeted with the Gateway Sign, a replica of the original sign built in the 1900s that greeted visitors at Central Avenue and C Street.

Just down the road from the replica sign, at the corner of Main Street and First Avenue NW, is the opulent Coleman Theatre built by wealthy local businessman George L. Coleman Sr. Coleman, who specialized in the lead and zinc mining industries, thought Miami needed its own theater, and he

The entryway to the Coleman Theatre in Miami, Oklahoma.

The ornate Coleman Theatre in Miami, Oklahoma.

The Coleman Theatre along Main Street in Miami, Oklahoma.

hired a Kansas City–based architecture firm to design the estimated $600,000 Spanish Colonial Revival–style building. A year after construction started, the elegant Coleman Theatre opened on April 18, 1929, to a capacity crowd of 1,600 who paid one dollar per seat to see the vaudeville performances.

The architecture of the building features twin bell towers on the south side and a spire-like bell tower in the center. Louis XV–style design elements accent the interior of the building. During its creation and completion in 1929, the Coleman Theatre was dubbed the most elaborate theater between Dallas and Kansas City and one of a few examples of buildings in the state of Oklahoma featuring the Spanish Colonial Revival style of architecture.

In addition to vaudeville acts, the theater featured early "talkie" pictures like *The Dummy* starring Fredric March, Jack Oakie and Ruth Chatterton.

The Coleman Theatre was placed on the National Register of Historic Places in 1983, and in 1989, the Coleman family donated the theater to the City of Miami. Volunteers worked to renovate and restore the theater to its original look and feel, including the Mighty Wurlitzer pipe organ that had been used to dazzle audiences for decades.

Today's theater-goers have an opportunity to step back in time when they visit the Coleman Theatre for a ballet, silent movie or community event. Route 66 enthusiasts and others are also able to tour the theater as they pass through Miami, pronounced My-Am-Uh and named after the Miami Indians. A barbershop and several storefronts line the outside of the Coleman Theatre.

Pawnee County

Ralston Corner Café

601 North Main Street, Ralston

Some of the first things visitors see when they drive into Ralston, a town in northeastern Pawnee County, are abandoned buildings lining Main Street. Overgrown weeds and shrubbery seem to sprout from atop some of the buildings, cascading all the way to the ground. Windows are missing in others, replaced by wooden boards. Among those once-distinguished buildings is the Ralston Opera House, a two-story structure constructed of local sandstone that included retail businesses on the ground floor and a live theater on the second floor.

Just a block away from what looks like a ghost town is the Ralston Corner Café, owned and operated by Roger and Cindy Green. Housed in a building that once was a post office, the family-style restaurant serves up steak sandwiches, mashed potatoes, pasta and more six days a week for Ralston residents, visitors from nearby communities and people from as far away as Tulsa and Oklahoma City.

"I thought this little town deserved a decent place," Cindy Green, fifty-seven, said as she and Roger prepared lunch in the back kitchen for hungry patrons.

The Greens opened the restaurant in the mid-2000s and pride themselves on being active community participants. They raise money each year around Christmas and throw a party for about 150 kids from Ralston and surrounding communities. The same thing takes place each spring for Easter.

"Anybody that knows about it and wants to come and eat, they can come and eat for free. It's a smorgasbord," said Roger Green, sixty-two, a veteran of the Vietnam War.

Dilapidated buildings line Main Street in Ralston, Oklahoma.

Roger and Cindy Green stand inside the kitchen of their restaurant, Ralston Corner Café, in Ralston, Oklahoma.

The Greens employ about twelve part-time workers at the restaurant, which features all homemade dishes, including chicken fries, mushrooms, onion rings and hand-cut ribeyes. Friday night at the Ralston Corner Café is fish night, and the restaurant sells out every week, Cindy Green said.

Running the restaurant has helped the couple meet a variety of people through the years. "These are real nice, caring folks who live here," Roger said, adding that if anyone in the community is ever in need, people help out.

It's no surprise that the population in Ralston has steadily declined. When Oklahoma became a state in 1907, 587 people called Ralston home. That increased to a high of 725 in 1930. After that, the population started to dwindle. By 1980, fewer than 500 people called the town home, and now only 330 residents live in Ralston.

Look no further than the boarded-up Main Street businesses to see why the community is having trouble attracting and keeping residents.

But Cindy and Roger Green think all that could change with the right perspective.

"This town is basically a poor town, but it could grow if people cared," Cindy said, adding that she would like to see Ralston have a library, park and museum for community members.

Payne County

Frank Eaton Home

750 North Main Street, Perkins

Originally located a block off Main Street, the home of Frank Eaton is now front and center for any visitors to this city of about 2,800 residents. Eaton was a cowboy, scout and deputy United States marshal, but what he is probably most well known for was being the inspiration for Oklahoma State University's Pistol Pete mascot.

Born in Hartford, Connecticut, in 1860, Eaton and his family relocated to Kansas when he was just a boy. At the age of eight, Eaton watched as his father was gunned down by a group of former Confederates.

"In '68, my father was called to the door and shot down like a darned mad dog by a bunch of, well, by a bunch of Missouri 'jebs.' Men that had been on the other side of the fence in the war, and there was six of them that killed him, there were six men killed him," Eaton said, according to a recording by the Oklahoma History Center.

A friend of the family instructed the young boy that he must avenge his father's death or be cursed and gave him a gun to use. Meanwhile, Eaton's mother and sister had moved to Indian Country in present-day Oklahoma in 1876, near the site of what is now Bartlesville. When Eaton was fifteen, he traveled to Fort Gibson to learn from the Sixth Cavalry soldiers but outshot everyone. It was there that Eaton reportedly earned his new name, Pistol Pete.

But even with his quick shot, it would take years for Eaton to track down each of his father's killers and avenge his death. Still a teenager, Eaton began serving as deputy United States marshal under Judge Isaac C. Parker, who

The home of Frank Eaton, inspiration for Oklahoma State University's Pistol Pete mascot, in Perkins, Oklahoma.

A statue of Frank Eaton in Perkins, Oklahoma.

was known as the "hanging judge" for the large number of hangings and death sentences he handed down.

In 1923, a group of students from Oklahoma Agricultural and Mechanical College decided that Eaton's Pistol Pete persona would make for a better school mascot than a tiger because, the students believed, Pistol Pete better represented Oklahoma's frontier spirit.

Eaton died in his sleep on April 8, 1958, at his home in Perkins at age ninety-seven. Nearly one thousand people turned out for his funeral.

Today, the iconic character with a thick black mustache, long braids, cowboy hat, jeans and—of course—a pistol at his side is synonymous with the Stillwater-based university.

University students and fans don't have to go far to see Eaton's home. Originally built around 1900, it still contains the original carpet as well as replicas of furniture and family photos. Pistol Pete memorabilia fills a glass enclosure at the entrance of the home, while family pictures and information about the man who inspired the Pistol Pete mascot hang on one wall.

Pittsburg County

Krebs Heritage Museum

Main Street, Krebs

The city of Krebs, located just outside of McAlester, seems to be known for two things—its Italian immigrant community and its deep ties to the mining industry.

About one hundred miners were killed during an explosion back in 1892 in this southeastern Oklahoma city. Drive throughout the community of two thousand and you may stumble upon a monument to the lost coal miners that was installed a century later. You'll also notice a variety of houses that have been converted to Italian restaurants, helping the city of Krebs earn the distinction of Oklahoma's "Little Italy."

One of the most well-known immigrants from Italy was Pietro Piegari, who moved with his family as a young boy from San Gregorio Magno to Krebs in 1903. At age eleven, young Pietro changed his name to Pete Prichard and, like many other immigrant men in the community—both young and old—went to work in the nearby mines. A decade later, Prichard almost died when a mine nearly caved in. His leg was so badly damaged that he was unable to return to work and turned his sights on other avenues to make money. One of those avenues was making and selling a homemade brew whose recipe had originated in Indian Territory and been passed on to Italian immigrants like Prichard and his family members.

Soon, English, Scottish, Irish and Italians who worked the coal mines started clamoring for the Choctaw beer following their hard days deep underground. It was only a matter of time before Prichard started cooking for his new patrons, and in 1925, Pete's Place officially opened in Prichard's home featuring all the hallmark dishes of a home-style Italian restaurant: spaghetti, meatballs and ravioli.

The restaurant is still going strong today and remains in the Prichard family. Its history and photos of its founding along with information about Pete Prichard are on display at one of the more than thirty family galleries at the Krebs Heritage Museum located along the town's now-sleepy business district on Main Street. Main Street was once home to an opera house and trolley route, but it's now the site of a few abandoned buildings, the museum, a post office and single-family homes.

The museum, which opened in 1996, was the brainchild of Gene DeFrange.

"He was a history buff and a patriot," Steve DeFrange said of his cousin. "He wanted to preserve history." Gene DeFrange started collecting the museum materials in his house, and when the collection got too large, he decided to create the museum.

The Heritage Museum features artifacts from different immigrant groups, servicemen and women and Native Americans. Coal mining equipment and tools are also featured along one wall, as well as a tuxedo worn by Congressman Carl Albert. Short in stature, the Democrat who served as the Speaker in the United States House of Representatives in the 1970s was known as the "little giant."

Though Gene DeFrange died in 2001, a board of directors continues to operate the museum.

Pontotoc County

McSwain Theatre

130 West Main Street, Ada

As he sat watching his first motion picture in 1910, Foster McSwain was instantly taken by the moving images before him. The well-known Ada businessman decided to start a career in show business—deep in the heart of Oklahoma. He purchased two local theaters before deciding to build his own.

From its earliest days showcasing silent films and vaudeville acts to hosting some of country music's biggest stars, the McSwain Theatre has continually reinvented itself and provided entertainment for generations of Oklahomans.

Built in 1920, the McSwain Theatre played host to the first showing of a movie with sound in Ada. Tickets back then cost about a quarter for adults and just ten cents for children.

In 1946, the McSwain hosted the world premiere of *Home of Oklahoma*, starring Roy Rogers, Dale Evans and Gabby Hayes. All three appeared at the premiere. Three years later, the film *Tulsa* held its premiere at the theater. Again, the event brought out some big names in Hollywood.

Admission to the McSwain increased to seventy-five cents by the 1960s as people lined up over the next few decades to see such films as *Psycho*, *The Godfather*, *Jaws* and *Star Wars*.

But hard times fell upon the grand theater in the 1980s, and the McSwain was forced to close its doors in July 1988. The reason? The historic theater couldn't compete with newer, large, multi-screen theater complexes.

More than seven decades after it opened, another local businessman, Paul Alford, sought to transform and bring new life to the McSwain in

The McSwain Theatre in Ada, Oklahoma.

the form of a variety show. Soon, a variety of performers began playing at the entertainment venue, including Ada native Blake Shelton and Pake McEntire and Susie McEntire, siblings of country singer and Oklahoma native Reba McEntire.

In 2002, the Chickasaw Nation purchased the McSwain and began running its operations. Extensive renovations at the theater took place, including adding an elevator, wheelchair-accessible seating and new, state-of-the-art sound and lighting systems. The stage area was redesigned to accommodate 574 people, while the second floor added a viewing area with a large video screen and an art gallery. The interior of the theater now features oak woodwork, high-quality tile and granite countertops, and the structural integrity of the building has been restored.

"Keeping history and culture alive is very important to the Chickasaw Nation," said Bill Anoatubby, the governor of the Chickasaw Nation, which is headquartered in Ada. "We thought it was important to preserve this historic theater because it has been an integral part of community life in Ada for decades. The McSwain has been a jewel in the crown of the city of Ada for decades, and we believe that will remain true for many years to come."

Nearly seventeen thousand people attended various events at the theater in 2012, including live family shows, concerts, summer movies, pageants and school programs. Anoatubby said the McSwain continues to remain a local icon for Ada.

"For decades, this theater has been a place where community members have made memories enjoying family entertainment and other events," he said. "Renovation of this historic structure is intended to restore that gathering place so future generations will have a special place to build their own memories."

Pottawatomie County

Ritz Theatre

10 West Main Street, Shawnee

With its large, vertical-hanging sign jutting down from the second floor and its old-fashioned marquee announcing the next big performance, the Ritz Theater is anything but modest.

Originally built as a dry goods store in 1897, it was transformed into a theater in 1913. Known as the Cozy, it was one of several theaters, opera houses and entertainment venues in the bustling community that once vied for the title of state capital.

Shawnee never did earn enough votes to become Oklahoma's capital—it lost out to Oklahoma City—but it did earn the right to become the county seat of Pottawatomie County in 1930 after that title moved from Tecumseh. The Cozy, meanwhile, earned the appreciation of locals. Around 1913, Jake Jones purchased the Cozy, and a decade later he renamed it the Ritz. It offered Shawnee residents their first chance to watch talkies, or movies with sound.

The Jones family stopped running the theater in the late 1980s and ended up donating the building to the city as a way to preserve the community's history and spur economic development in the downtown area.

In recent years, various musicians, artists and other entertainers have performed at the theater through the Society for Revitalization of Downtown Shawnee.

The Ritz is also known for a far spookier reason. Some people claim that the Ritz's longtime projectionist, Leo Montgomery, haunts the building. Montgomery worked at the theater for more than fifty years until he died from a heart attack while a movie played in 1965.

The Ritz Theatre in Shawnee, Oklahoma.

Pushmataha County

Gailbert's Whitetail Run

716 East Main Street, Antlers

As the deer capital of the world—so say the signs that greet visitors to Antlers, Oklahoma—seeing stuffed deer heads and antlers hanging from the wall of this all-purpose store that offers specialty foods and antique furniture doesn't seem that out of the ordinary.

What sets Gailbert's Whitetail Run apart from other Main Street stores in small cities and towns across Oklahoma is found just outside the front door on the store's front porch.

A life-size Chewbacca mannequin covered from head to toe in long, flowing brown hair and a menacing face wears a jean skirt with pink ruffles. The sight is just enough to get headstrong travelers to stop, pull over and decide that Gailbert's is worthy of their time.

Once inside, they won't be disappointed. Gailbert's Whitetail Run offers an assortment of jams, jellies, salsas and fudge for sale as well as kitchenware, furniture and other antique items.

Roger Mills County

Hammon Park

Main Street, Hammon

Monuments play an important role in honoring the people of Hammon. Two monuments in the town's park along Main Street pay tribute to the local men and women who have served in the military. One lists all of the local community members who have served in various wars over the years, while a second one, dedicated in 1985, just a few short strides away, has a bell on top and a simple description: "In memory to veterans of all wars."

Both are in close proximity to a third monument at the park, which commemorates one of the most tragic and well-known events of Hammon's history. On April 4, 1934, rising waters from the Washita River—the result of fourteen inches of rain falling in a matter of hours—overtook the town, killing seventeen of the more than seven hundred people who lived in Hammon at the time.

Many of those killed were family members. In fact, of the seventeen people who died, all had one of four last names—Adams, Bush, Fenter or Taylor.

Floyd Bush, then eighty-four, recounted to the *Oklahoman* in a 2007 story about losing his mother, father and young sister in the flood. Bush and his older brother, Woodrow, managed to survive by holding tightly to a tree for fourteen hours before rescuers reached them. Another brother, Elvin, had tried to run to a nearby neighbor's house to retrieve a horse in hopes of saving the family, but it was too late by the time he returned. The bodies of Floyd's father, mother and twelve-year-old sister were all found by searchers.

"We never really talked about that night afterward," he told the *Oklahoman* from his home in Texas. "I never really talked about it with my kids either."

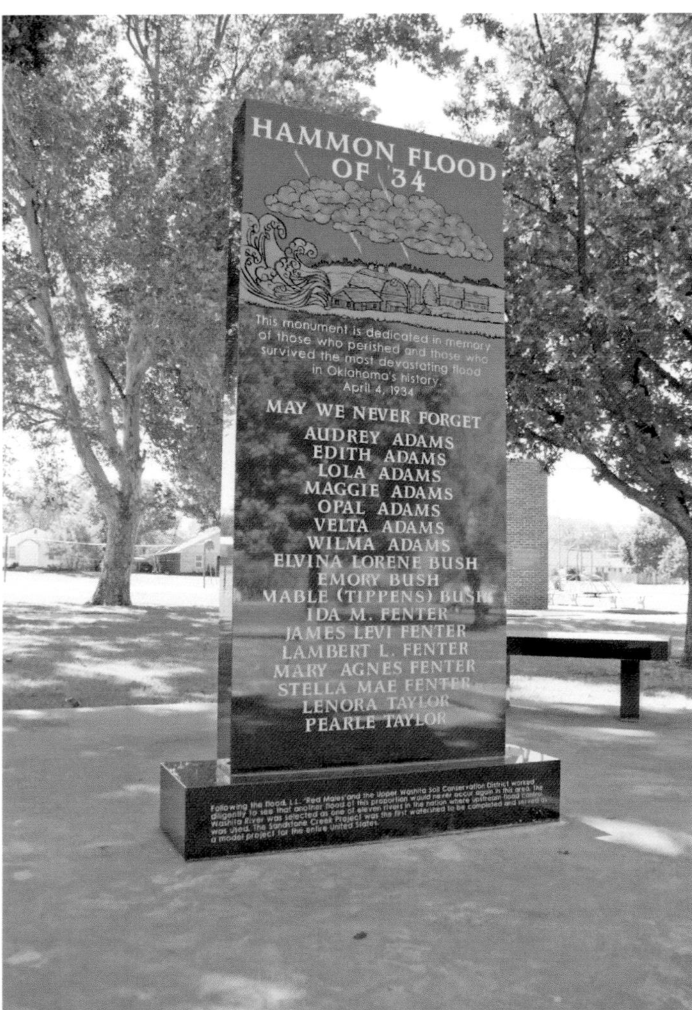

A monument honoring flood victims at a park on Main Street in Hammon, Oklahoma.

An inscription on the monument recognizes the effect the flood had on the town and its people. The names of each of the seventeen people killed are listed on the monument along with a dedication: "This monument is dedicated in memory of those who perished and those who survived the most devastating flood in Oklahoma's history. April 4, 1934. May we never forget."

Rogers County

Arlene Van Brunt

Main Street, Tiawah

It's just a lovely place if you want quietness. It's not like town.
—Arlene Van Brunt

Arlene Van Brunt thoroughly enjoys living in her home along Main Street in the tiny community of Tiawah. It's peaceful and a slower pace of life yet only a few minutes' drive to Claremore, the largest city and county seat of Rogers County. The hills overlooking Tiawah are breathtaking, and in the fall, the leaves on the trees transform into some of the most beautiful orange, yellow and brown hues.

But there is one complaint she has about living on the influential-sounding street: the ditch on the edge of her property, just near the road.

The narrow excavation isn't deep enough, she said, and water overflows and floods the road and her neighbor's yard across the street. Worse yet, when the water recedes, it remains stagnant and attracts mosquitoes and other pesky insects.

"I'm ashamed of that because they don't make it deeper or nothing, and you call in and they don't care how it looks," the seventy-eight-year-old mother and grandmother said, later adding: "It's a Main Street. It should be taken care of."

But the community is tiny—only 189 people call it home—and it's considered a census-designated place, meaning it's not legally incorporated. Main Street is one of the few roads in Tiawah, and it's made up of about six houses, including Van Brunt's.

Arlene Van Brunt and her dog, Lollipop, stand outside her Main Street home in Tiawah, Oklahoma.

Van Brunt moved to the community from Tulsa with her husband seventeen years ago to be closer to their daughter. Initially, she said, she disliked the idea, but her husband fell in love with the community instantly. Tragically, he had a heart attack three days after they moved to the home on Main Street and died. Since then, Arlene Van Brunt has been trying to keep busy. After retiring from her job as a school janitor, she started focusing on her home. She'll work in the yard and do little odd paint jobs on it at times, she said.

About two years ago, she got a new family member—a Shih Tzu named Lollipop that keeps her company and helps prevent her from feeling lonely.

"I just love her to pieces, but I didn't want another dog," Van Brunt said about acquiring Lollipop. Her granddaughter's friend wasn't able to keep her and was in need of a new home for Lollipop. Upon meeting her, Van Brunt bonded quickly. The rest, they say, is history. "She keeps me a lot of company, and I'll talk to her."

Although her daughter has moved out of Tiawah, Van Brunt for the most part thinks she'll stick around until she moves into a retirement community.

"We have no problems," she said.

Seminole County

Seminole Producer

121 North Main Street, Seminole

The *Seminole Producer* started with little expectation. Founders Sadie and James T. Jackson started the daily newspaper in 1927 plagued, James Jackson would later write, with trouble and uncertainty.

On March 1, 1927, the first day the newspaper was to be published, there were no subscribers or advertisers. It didn't matter. In fact, Sadie Jackson had earlier predicted—and encouraged—such an outcome when she convinced James Jackson that the *Producer* should be a daily newspaper instead of a semi-weekly or weekly. "Let's make it a daily; we'll go broke and get out of here quicker that way," James Jackson wrote that Sadie had said, according to an account on the *Producer* website.

By midmorning on that March day, though, the luck for the two and the newspaper was already turning around. The superintendent of schools arrived at the newspaper office and bought a one-year subscription, increasing its circulation to one.

Less than a year later, the *Producer* staff exposed wrongdoings by the county's law enforcement agencies, ultimately forcing eleven deputy sheriffs from their jobs and two constables to resign. A third constable was fired after filing a libel suit against the *Producer*, the newspaper's first such lawsuit, though not its last.

With new attention brought to the newspaper, circulation and advertising money increased, meaning the Jacksons didn't get the quick exit they had hoped for. They ran the *Producer* until 1946.

James Jackson said there were four things every community needed in order to grow and prosper: churches, good schools, banks with "deep-rooted interest in the community" and an aggressive and fearless newspaper. Without all four, he said, a community would not survive. Together, he and Sadie provided Seminole and its people with one of the four integral parts of a prosperous town.

Brothers Milt and Tom Phillips bought the *Seminole Producer* in 1946, having already been involved in the newspaper business for years. They combined the *Producer* with the *Seminole County News* in 1948, and in 1950, they purchased the *Wewoka Times* and the *Wewoka Democrat* to combine into one daily newspaper. The plan had been to create one central printing plant in Wewoka, but Tom died in 1956 after being diagnosed with cancer. Milt Phillips then sold minority interests to three key staff members. Later, one of those employees sold back his interest when he moved and another died. Stu Phillips acquired the stock of the third employee and became the sole owner in 2004. He also publishes two other newspapers in Seminole County, the *Wewoka Times* and the *Konawa Leader*.

The *Seminole Producer* is a five-day-a-week publication with a circulation of more than five thousand featuring local community members. Residents recently featured include a set of ninety-five-year-old twins, a family who has been involved in banking for four generations and a man starting a cowboy church. Local sports events as well as wedding and engagement announcements are also featured.

The *Seminole Producer* has also continued its role as local watchdog, Stu Phillips said, though that role makes it difficult to retain friends sometimes in a community of about 7,500 people.

"In big cities, writers may never see the person they write about," he said. "Here we see them, often several times a week. I've lost several good friends over the years because I had to do what was right as a journalist and not pull a punch for a friend."

Sequoyah County

General Lee's Haircuts and Perms

Main Street, Muldrow

Randy Lee is one of those colorful small-town characters who can put a smile on your face. Lee, the owner of General Lee's Haircuts and Perms in the eastern Oklahoma town of Muldrow, population 3,460, came about his profession in a most peculiar way: as the singer and guitar player of an Ohio-based band, he was asked to cut the hair of his fellow bandmate, and he soon learned he had a knack for it. Though he hasn't given up his rock star dreams—he still plays in his church band—Lee has turned his attention to hair, spending the past three decades cutting and styling the young and old.

"I enjoy the people even after all these years," the sixty-year-old said after finishing a cut one Saturday morning in his small shop along Main Street.

Pricing at General Lee's is simple: ten dollars for haircuts, forty dollars for perms. Customers, Lee said, come from all over the community and nearby Arkansas for his expert skills.

Another draw for potential clients? The shop's look and feel. Don't expect an upscale salon complete with granite finishings and high-fashion photos hanging from the walls. General Lee's is all about character. His family members decided to cover his walls one weekend in the 1990s when he was out of town with Coca-Cola wallpaper. The fascination with the iconic beverage caught on, and soon customers and residents began giving Lee their memorabilia, including old Coke bottles, a toy truck with the Coke logo and Coke signs.

Randy Lee, owner of General Lee's Haircuts and Perms, poses next to his Coca-Cola memorabilia in his shop in Muldrow, Oklahoma.

"Coke should do something for me as much as I advertise for them," Lee said, only somewhat joking it seemed.

So, there must be a fun story behind how Lee became such a Coke fanatic, right? Not exactly.

"Actually, I like Pepsi," he said, chuckling.

Stephens County

Historical Markers

Main Street, Duncan

They say you shouldn't look down when you walk. But in Duncan, it's the best way to learn about the history of this south-central Oklahoma city.

Tidbits of trivia and history about the community are engraved in the sidewalks lining Duncan's Main Street. Though the history of how the Main Street steppingstones came to be seems to have been lost over the years—even current officials at Main Street Duncan, which was in charge of the sidewalk program, couldn't offer many concrete details—the pieces offer a unique way to learn about the city's history.

The Main Street Duncan program, created in 1986, was one of the first Main Street programs started in Oklahoma to help revitalize and promote Main Streets. The influential role Main Street plays is actually written on one of the many stones lining Duncan's thoroughfare, which includes a 1950s-style escalator at an antique store and an old-fashioned soda fountain at a drugstore:

> *The importance of downtowns is about more than retail business. It is about maintaining a cohesive area where citizens can come together in times of joy or strife. It is the glue which holds a community together.*

The historical markers were bought by individual property owners or Duncan residents in memory of family members or friends.

One four-stone marker tells the story of how oil shaped the growth of Duncan, from the town's first oil well in 1918 named in honor of a Native

Historical markers line Main Street in Duncan, Oklahoma.

American to Erle P. Halliburton founding his namesake company, the company's subsequent growth and impact on Duncan's population over the years and the company's eventual decline. "Oil was the major factor in our growth and responsible for the presence of many influential citizens," the marker reads, noting that Duncan's population swelled from 3,463 in 1920 to 21,732 in 1990.

Other markers along the street share the admiration many have for the community. Wayne Holden, a six-term mayor of Duncan who died in 2009, and his wife, Marie, shared their fondness for the Duncan community:

> *As members of the First Baptist Church its members provided our family with spiritual guidance and Christian love. Halliburton Company provided for the temporal needs of our family by being a good employer. The Duncan Public Schools system provided a good education for our children. The city of Duncan provided a good place for us to raise our family.*

And still other markers include surprising pieces of trivia or little-known facts that would have more than likely been lost over time if not for such a permanent record. For example, the first wedding in Duncan occurred on February 28, 1892; the original city hall was built in 1909 for $6,870; and on April Fools' Day in 1913, eight members of the high school senior class dressed in rags and ran from the school. A paddle welcomed them back to school upon their return.

Texas County

Pioneer Days Parade and Cultural Festivities

Main Street, Guymon

The Oklahoma Panhandle is known for its pioneer spirit. Before becoming a part of Oklahoma Territory, the land was known as No Man's Land, a lawless haven for rough-and-tumble outlaws trying to escape crimes and adventurous land squatters trying to start anew. Later, during the grim Depression era of the 1930s, residents were forced to withstand a period of severe drought and blinding dust storms known as the Dust Bowl. Times were tough for the people of the Panhandle, and there were many reasons to give up. But many kept on working and living as best they could, and around that time, local leaders in Guymon started looking for ways to entice visitors to the area as well as a reason to celebrate despite the difficult times.

Leaders settled on the idea of a celebration called Pioneer Days, featuring a world-class rodeo, carnival and parade along Main Street. Held the first weekend of May, the festivities coincide with the anniversary of the 1890 signing of the Organic Act, which placed the area known as No Man's Land into Oklahoma Territory.

Seventy years later, people with pioneer spirits from near and far are still descending on the city of 11,400, and the celebration is still going strong in the Panhandle's largest community.

But in recent years, as the demographics of this Panhandle community change dramatically, new festivals have started popping up along Guymon's Main Street. While the events are still paying homage to Guymon's history, they are also meant to applaud the cultures of the city's newest residents. In the past few decades, the number of Hispanic residents living in the

The Spanish language is seen on signs and storefronts on Guymon's Main Street.

Two dancers from the Alma Folklorica Dancers of Oklahoma group perform at the Guymon Fiesta along Main Street. *Courtesy of Main Street Guymon.*

area has exploded—more than half of the city's population is Hispanic or Latino compared to less than 10 percent in the entire state of Oklahoma, according to the 2010 United States Census. A large number of immigrants from Africa have also started moving to the Guymon area to work in a hog processing plant.

Nowhere is this demographic change more noticeable than on Guymon's Main Street, where about half the stores are owned by Hispanic businesspeople, said Melyn Johnson with the Guymon Main Street organization. Signs are written in both English and Spanish on many storefront windows, and store hours are more apt to coincide with the owner's native land—opening at noon and closing at 8:00 p.m., instead of the customary 9:00 a.m. to 5:00 p.m. mostly seen across the United States.

Johnson said the changing hours have made shopping easier for some residents because they are now able to shop along Main Street after getting off work. In August, the town hosts a gala in recognition of the African immigrants. The event, called Azuma: An African Celebration, celebrates the cultures of several African countries through food, dancing and storytelling. The following month, Main Street is home to the Guymon Fiesta, which honors the area's Hispanic residents and the period of time when the Panhandle was under Mexican and Spanish control.

"We had a lot of new Hispanic people in town and there was friction," Johnson said. "The arts and a celebration brings barriers down faster than anything."

Tillman County

Tanglewood Motel

1121 South Main Street, Frederick

Founded in 1981, this twenty-six-room motel located on the south end of Frederick's Main Street was originally built as a way to help keep a fading restaurant open.

"We built it [Tanglewood] for the restaurant—to help the restaurant—and the motel made more money than the restaurant," Tanglewood Motel founder Sue Harper said. She eventually sold the restaurant, and it has been turned into a Mexican establishment.

Tanglewood remains in the family, though. Sue Harper continues to work at the motel, but she's not the owner anymore. She sold it to her daughter and son-in-law recently.

So who stays at the motel—featuring an indoor fish and game cleaning station as well as outdoor grills and picnic tables, laundry service and RV hookups—in this southwestern Oklahoma city of fewer than four thousand people?

"Certainly not the tourists," Harper said with a laugh, adding that the motel is seldom at capacity. "You know, it's either business, a crew or someone working here. [There are] very few just visitors."

Frederick, established in 1902, was once known as Gosnell. When the Blackwell, Enid and Southern Railroad was considering building its line through the area, a representative from the railroad asked to change the name of Gosnell to Frederick, in honor of the son of railroad director Jacob C. Van Blarcom. In exchange, a depot was placed in town.

Though Frederick may not attract that many visitors now, more than a century ago it drew one of the biggest names in the country.

President Theodore Roosevelt chose Frederick as his vacation spot in 1905 to wolf hunt with local resident John "Jack" Abernathy. Nearly six thousand people welcomed the president into town on that April day as he spoke about his hope of Oklahoma becoming a state, according to a story in the *Frederick Enterprise* newspaper. Two years later, Oklahoma became the forty-sixth state in the Union.

Two of Abernathy's sons, Bud and Temple, made headlines of their own in 1909. Just five and nine years old at the time, the two boys headed off on their own to New Mexico Territory on horseback. A year later, the two boys took their adventures further. They rode by horseback from Frederick to New York City to greet their old friend, former President Roosevelt, as he returned home from work in Africa. Media heralded the two boys, calling them "the little cowboys from Oklahoma." Their ride home to Oklahoma was just as noteworthy. Instead of riding on horses, they drove home in a bright red Brush Runabout. The Abernathy boys are celebrated for their adventurous spirit each year in Frederick with a festival.

Present-day visitors to the area can catch a small glimpse of what life was like during Roosevelt's visit to the city at the Pioneer Townsite Museum, a representation of a 1920s-era town site. It includes the Frisco Depot, where President Roosevelt's train arrived during the historic visit; a 1902 school; a farmhouse and church dating back to the 1920s; and other artifacts.

Tulsa County

Cain's Ballroom

423 North Main Street, Tulsa

Owning and operating one of the oldest and most storied music venues in Oklahoma is a family affair for brothers Chad and Hunter Rodgers and their parents.

The Rodgers family purchased Cain's Ballroom in October 2002 within days of learning that the historic venue was up for sale. Since then, Cain's has helped reinvigorate downtown Tulsa and its music scene, to the point that the venue is regularly ranked among the top club venues in the country for ticket sales.

"We knew it was a landmark, but I don't know if we honestly knew it had the reputation it did in the music industry," said Chad Rodgers, Cain's general manager.

Built in 1924, the sandstone building was constructed as either a garage or automobile dealership by one of Tulsa's founders, Tate Brady, a prominent businessman who became the center of controversy nearly ninety years after his death. In 2013, city councilors decided to change Brady Street—named for the one-time Tulsa leader—after it was discovered that Tate Brady had been a member of the Ku Klux Klan. Rather than do away completely with its name—a potentially costly endeavor—councilmembers opted to just change who it was named for. In this case, they renamed it M.B. Brady, for American Civil War photographer Mathew Brady.

Various dance schools were housed in the building Tate Brady built in the early years, including Cain's Dancing Academy, where people went to learn the latest dance craze. It later became known as the regular stomping

Concertgoers mill about outside Cain's Ballroom in Tulsa, Oklahoma.

ground for Bob Wills, whose western swing brought out hundreds on both weekends and weeknights. Photos of Wills and other artists now adorn the modern-day Cain's Ballroom

Cain's went dark at various times over the years, and by the time the Rodgers family purchased it, it had started to become rundown to the point that buckets were being used to catch water seeping through the roof.

It would have been easy to tear Cain's Ballroom down and put up something else, Chad Rodgers said, but the family decided instead to purchase it, shut it down and work to restore it. They put in a new stage along with new bathrooms and had new plumbing installed.

Nearly six months later, in the fall of 2003, Cain's reopened to a sold-out Dwight Yoakam show and a new generation of musicians and fans eager to spend a few hours of their time in the 1,800-capacity venue.

Chad and Hunter, who had no previous experience running a music venue, learned over the years how to book acts, though Chad will still tell you that booking nearly every show is a gamble.

"When we book a show, we don't honestly know with any given true guarantee that it's going to sell this many tickets at least," he said. "Every show is kind of a coin toss."

The brothers, who are both in their thirties and also run a booking and production company called Doc Rock Productions, have learned to leave their emotions at the door and book bands and artists based on the best research they have before them.

"Ultimately, we run it as though it's any business," Chad said. "Just because I like so and so...doesn't mean they're going to sell tickets or bring in people and make it a decent show for us."

That mindset seems to be working with Cain's, which is one of the top venues of its size in the country.

"We just want to continue on and hopefully keep Tulsa, Cain's and Oklahoma on the map as far as the eyes of all of the artists and entertainment people out there," Chad said.

Wagoner County

Wagoner City Historical Museum

122 South Main Street, Wagoner

Hundreds of historical dresses, shoes, hats and purses—some dating back to the 1800s—showcase Wagoner's history as the first incorporated city in Indian Territory at the city's Historical Museum.

Located along the community's once-bustling Main Street, the museum is filled with clothing, historical documents, antiques and other possessions donated or on loan by the people who lived and worked in Wagoner over the years.

"The clothing has all been worn by people in Wagoner, the furniture is out of their homes. There is nothing that I know of that has been donated by anyone out of the county," said museum director Chris Fultz.

Wagoner, the seat of the county by the same name, is located in northeastern Oklahoma. Once a hub of commerce and a variety of industries like tobacco, cotton and lumber, the city at one time was home to five railroad lines and five hotels that remained at capacity because of all the visiting businessmen in town, Fultz said. One of the first cotton gins in the area was located in Wagoner, as well as a bottling plant for purity soft drinks in flavors like orange and grape.

The community, named for Henry Wagoner, a dispatcher with the Katy Railroad, even vied for the title of state capital but lost out to Guthrie, which held on to the title for just three years before it moved to Oklahoma City.

Over time, Fultz said, apathy and a loss of interest set in, and the booming business atmosphere waned as the commerce slowly moved away. "The townspeople just kind of lost interest in things," she said. "They didn't want it to grow. They didn't want the town to change, and so businesses, which had been flourishing, a lot of the businesses just dried up."

Just in the past decade, about six different buildings along Main Street have shuttered, forcing the young people graduating from high school to seek work and opportunities elsewhere, away from the city of 8,300. "The townspeople don't seem to want to grow, and they don't seem to understand that if you don't grow, that means you die," Fultz said.

Still, the history of Wagoner, home to the first public school in Indian Territory, is alive and well because of the City Historical Museum. The dress collection takes visitors on a visual journey through time. One dress, a long-sleeved, high-neck piece with a bustle back and a full skirt, was worn by a lady who was in mourning for two years following the death of her husband. Called the "Mourning Dress," the piece of clothing dates back to 1870. Other clothing items include dresses with lace bodices and silk skirts and poodle dresses, the popular 1950s-era outfit favored by women for its wide felt skirt, often in bright shades, that swung around when dancing.

Many of the museum's pieces have been appraised for thousands of dollars, including a furniture set that is composed of a walnut bed and vanity, cradle, two chairs and a table. One handmade quilt is apparently worth $30,000.

"We just have a really nice collection," Fultz said.

Washington County

Foster's Grocery

Corner of Main and Ochelata Streets, Ochelata

Few homes or businesses are located on Main Street in this community of about 425 people in northeast Oklahoma named for a former principal chief of the Cherokee Nation.

Instead, Ochelata Street—a north–south street that bisects Main—acts as the main thoroughfare through the town located about thirty miles south of the Kansas state line. Ochelata's post office and several businesses are all located along the street, and at the corner of Main and Ochelata Streets sits Foster's Grocery, a grocery store and gas station serving as a hub for the community.

Started by Danny Foster with his wife, Judy, in 1976, Foster's Grocery serves as the one-stop shop for residents in need of drinks, food to munch on or even live bait. Foster, who was born in Oklahoma City, moved with his parents to Ochelata as an infant. After spending his youth in the small community, Foster headed to college out of town and began a teaching career before returning to the small community. Originally named Otis, the community was renamed Ochelata in 1899 for Charles Thompson, a former principal chief of the Cherokee Nation whose Cherokee name was Oochalata.

Though Danny Foster died at age sixty-nine in 2008, his legacy lives on at the store. A marker outside commemorates the businessman, community leader, historian, teacher and friend.

In 2009, Ochelata lost some of its history when a fire destroyed one of the town's oldest buildings.

The building was at one time the town's only bar, called Moon Glow Hut, and where people gathered for a fun time on a Saturday night before it shut down. It then became storage and housed many of the community's oldest historical photographs and documents. But an early morning fire that authorities believe was intentionally set destroyed all the mementos, which Mayor Sid Barnes said was a setback for the community and its residents.

"We're all kind of shocked and all devastated. You know, it's a little disheartening that we lose a landmark," Barnes told Tulsa TV station KOTV.

Washita County

Cordell Beacon

115 East Main Street, Cordell

It's a very vibrant industry for this particular market. We're giving them news they can't get anywhere else.
—Zonelle Rainbolt, editor of the Cordell Beacon

As the oldest continually operated business in Washita County in western Oklahoma, the *Cordell Beacon* provides residents of Cordell as well as surrounding communities in Washita with local news they can't get anywhere else—the upcoming pumpkin festival, the local high school homecoming festivities, blood drives and more.

"We're right there front and center taking pictures at the pep assembly and the parade and coronation. We do their sports teams. We cover city council meetings. Who else is going to do that?" asked Rainbolt, who has been editor of the weekly newspaper since 2000.

Originally based in Cloud Chief, which was the county seat of Washita until 1900, the *Beacon* moved to New Cordell when it became the county seat. (The city was previously located a few miles away but was moved to its current location around 1900. It became known as New Cordell, though today most people just call it Cordell.) The newspaper, which has four full-time staff members and three part-time employees and a circulation of about three thousand, is "blanketed" across the county and mailed to subscribers in other states. There's also a website and Facebook page, Rainbolt said.

"I always think of the paper as the community's cheerleader," she said. "There are bad things that happen and bad news sells newspapers, but

Cordell's Main Street, including the office of the *Cordell Beacon*.

you're also the one that keeps people focused on what's happening in the community."

Several years ago, the newspaper changed from a Thursday publication to a Wednesday publication at the request of local advertisers. The grocery store wanted ads to start on Wednesday, Rainbolt said.

Rainbolt, who was an English teacher before becoming editor, said working at the newspaper requires passion because of the long hours.

"And you've got to be willing to be a lightning rod," she said. "If there is ever a controversial issue, then you find yourself trying to walk that really narrow line between them and be neutral and yet, almost everyone perceives you have a favorite. And sometimes you do, and you work even harder to be neutral and it shows—your writing is not quite as interesting."

Small communities also breed rumors, so Rainbolt said it's imperative for reporters to do their own digging when they get a tip. Oftentimes, she said, a community member will come to the newspaper with what they believe is a juicy tip, only to find out that the big "get" isn't so newsworthy after all.

Sometimes people do offer interesting tidbits that lead to stories—sometimes even about themselves. One time, Rainbolt said, a woman charged with embezzling money pleaded not guilty in an open courtroom at the Washita County Courthouse. Afterward, she headed straight across the street to the newspaper's office and confessed to Rainbolt on the record that she did, in fact, embezzle the money. She eventually pleaded guilty to the charge.

Another time Rainbolt said she took justice into her own hands was when she felt two brothers skirted the law. The men had been convicted of child-sex-related crimes in Washita County but because of a loophole did not have to register as sex offenders after serving their sentence. When the brothers moved back to Cordell, Rainbolt took a photograph of their house and published it along with the crimes they were convicted of committing.

"We registered for them," Rainbolt said. The men eventually left the area, and reaction was mixed to how the editor handled the situation. "Some were grateful, and some thought I was not as forgiving as I should be—that they had paid their debt when in fact they had not."

Cordell, Rainbolt said, has survived better than some small communities. The population remains steady at a little more than 2,900 people. People haven't left, but there's also not a lot drawing younger people back to the city once they graduate from college, she said.

Main Street remains fairly vibrant, she said, though it has its struggles. "Main Streets are suffering a little bit because of retail, and that's true across the United States. The retail has been pushed out by the big box stores."

Woods County

Freedom Bank Robbery and Shootout

Main Street, Freedom

Cowpokes and saloon girls may not be a regular sight along Main Street in Freedom, but that won't stop visitors from feeling like they have been transported back in time to the rough-and-tumble era of the Old West.

With just a few hundred people residing in town, Freedom could have been like any other small community in Oklahoma: quaint, slow-paced and simple. Though Freedom may have some of those qualities, it stands out on its own. Community members realized a few decades ago that they needed to do more to survive, so they concocted an idea to bring the Old West to them and the people who visit. Cedar wood now covers every storefront along with simple block letters denoting the bank, museum, saloon and other stores, giving the street the look and feel of an authentic cow town.

"We're one of those towns that should have dried up and blown away by now," said Brett Smith, who was president of the Freedom State Bank—which was the first to convert to the western motif back in 1972—until the bank closed in 2014. Soon, other stores on the street joined in the fun, and Main Street in Freedom looked like a set straight out of a Wild West movie.

But long before Main Street became a rousing cow town lookalike, Freedom had already started saluting its western heritage with a rodeo and reunion for the old-time cowhands.

The three-day Freedom Rodeo and Cowhand reunion takes place in August. It features a chuck wagon feed with the same foods it did when it started in the 1930s—beef, beans and black coffee.

The town of Freedom, Oklahoma, holds a staged bank robbery and shootout along its Main Street every year.

About six thousand people turn out over the three days—a number, Smith said, that is "not too bad for a town of three hundred."

In the early 1990s, the chamber of commerce decided to further capitalize on its Wild West identity and added a mock bank robbery and shootout on Main Street.

Though it doesn't take place at high noon, the staged event features all the characters you'd expect to see: merchants, saloon girls, a butcher, an outlaw gang and posse and more.

With just one rehearsal before the real event under their belt each year, the more than thirty volunteers—all from Freedom or the surrounding area—could expect anything to happen. But Smith, who directs the show, said most are old hands at making the Wild West come to life.

Woodward County

Woodward Arts Theatre

818 Main Street, Woodward

A recent addition to the National Register of Historic Places, the Woodward Arts Theatre along bustling Main Street stands out not only for its unique contributions to keeping the arts alive in this town of twelve thousand but also for its unique architecture style among commercial buildings.

Built in 1929 as a motion picture theater, the two-story building features Italian Renaissance styles and a marquee out front typical of movie theaters in the 1940s and 1950s. The two brothers who built the structure, D. Vance Terry and Ben Terry, weren't completely sold on the idea of motion pictures, so they made sure the theater had all the necessities to host vaudeville acts as well, including dressing rooms, an orchestra pit and a loft to raise and lower curtains and backdrops.

Though it opened in the same year the crash on Wall Street set the stage for the Great Depression, the Woodward Theatre was still able to attract many theater-goers—both those with excess wealth to spare and those on a shoestring budget—eager for entertainment.

A tornado that ripped through Woodward on April 9, 1947—killing more than one hundred people, making it the deadliest tornado in Oklahoma's history—had surprisingly little impact on the theater's vitality. Other parts of town were decimated completely, but the theater had little damage, though the marquee was destroyed.

Volunteers worked to restore the historic theater in 1981, and in 2004, the balcony was restored, increasing the seating capacity in the

A marquee outside the Woodward Arts Theatre displays an upcoming performance.

theater to five hundred. The Woodward Arts Council now holds a summer arts camp, concert series, dinner theater performances and other shows at the theater. It was listed on the National Register of Historic Places in 2008.

Bibliography

B&O Cash Store. Temple Museum Association. http://www.angelfire.com/ok5/museumtemple/bocash.html#topp (accessed March 1, 2014).

Baker, Jack D. "Westville." Encyclopedia of Oklahoma History and Culture. http://digital.library.okstate.edu/encyclopedia/entries/W/WE020.html (accessed April 11, 2014).

Barnard, Robert J. "Shawnee." Encyclopedia of Oklahoma History and Culture. http://digital.library.okstate.edu/encyclopedia/entries/S/SH012.html (accessed October 25, 2013).

Black Theater of Ardmore. National Register of Historic Places nomination form. http://www.ocgi.okstate.edu/shpo/nhrpdfs/84002978.pdf (accessed February 2, 2014).

Break, Richard W. "Pain of Bank Robbery Murders Pulls Geronimo Together." *Oklahoman*, June 2, 1985. http://newsok.com/pain-of-bank-robbery-murders-pulls-geronimo-together/article/2110620 (accessed October 3, 2013).

Buffington Hotel. National Register of Historic Places inventory form. http://www.ocgi.okstate.edu/shpo/nhrpdfs/84002929.pdf (accessed April 11, 2014).

Burnett Mansion. "About." http://burnettmansion.info/welcome/ (accessed October 17, 2013).

Butler's Antiques. Historic Hotel Love pamphlet. August 10, 2013.

Carrels, Mike. "Coffee House Plan Wins Biz Competitions." *Muskogee Phoenix*, June 20, 2012. http://www.muskogeephoenix.com/x1426062404/Coffee-house-plan-wins-biz-competition (accessed November 21, 2013).

———. "Renovation Brings More to Main Street." *Muskogee Phoenix*, October 7, 2012. http://www.muskogeephoenix.com/local/x1149575939/Renovation-brings-more-to-Main-Street (accessed November 21, 2013).

Cheatham, Gary J. "Delaware." Encyclopedia of Oklahoma History and Culture. http://digital.library.okstate.edu/encyclopedia/entries/D/DE009.html (accessed November 4, 2013).

"Circus City USA." City of Hugo and Choctaw County. http://www.hugo2choctawcountyok.com/155/Circus-City-USA (accessed May 10, 2014).

Coleman Theatre. Promotional pamphlet. October 31, 2013.

County Courthouse of Oklahoma. National Register of Historic Places inventory form. http://www.ocgi.okstate.edu/shpo/nhrpdfs/84003148.pdf (accessed October 23, 2013).

Craig County Genealogical Society. "Bluejacket." Encyclopedia of Oklahoma History and Culture. http://digital.library.okstate.edu/encyclopedia/entries/B/BL015.html (accessed November 7, 2013).

Davis Santa Fe Depot. National Register of Historic Places registration form. http://www.ocgi.okstate.edu/shpo/nhrpdfs/94001507.pdf (accessed November 20, 2013).

Dean, Michael. "Frank Eaton." Oklahoma Historical Society, November 1, 2011. http://www.okhistory.org/about/transcript.php?episodedate=2010-11-01 (accessed October 4, 2013).

Denny, Dale. "Jay." Encyclopedia of Oklahoma History and Culture. http://digital.library.okstate.edu/encyclopedia/entries/J/JA014.html (accessed November 19, 2013)

Electric Park Pavillion. National Register of Historic Places inventory nomination form. http://www.ocgi.okstate.edu/shpo/nhrpdfs/76001563.pdf (accessed October 3, 2013).

Elmore City Chamber of Commerce. "About." http://elmorecitychamber.com/about.htm (accessed October 3, 2013).

Evaige, Wanda Jo. "Frederick." Encyclopedia of Oklahoma History and Culture. http://digital.library.okstate.edu/encyclopedia/entries/F/FR011.html (accessed October 7, 2013).

Everett, Dianna. "Garber." Encyclopedia of Oklahoma History and Culture. http://digital.library.okstate.edu/encyclopedia/entries/g/ga010.html (accessed November 13, 2013)

———. "Mulhall." Encyclopedia of Oklahoma History and Culture. http://digital.library.okstate.edu/encyclopedia/entries/M/MU005.html (accessed October 3, 2013).

———. "Roserock." Encyclopedia of Oklahoma History and Culture. http://digital.library.okstate.edu/encyclopedia (accessed October 3, 2013).

Farmers and Merchants National Bank. National Register of Historic Places nomination form. http://www.ocgi.okstate.edu/shpo/nhrpdfs/84003085.pdf (accessed November 14, 2013).

Find a Grave. Obituary notice for Danny Eugene Foster. http://www.findagrave.com/cgi-bin/fg.cgi?page=gr&GRid=84146028 (accessed November 6, 2013).

Frank Eaton Historic Home. http://www.eatonhome.org/ (accessed October 4, 2013).

Frederick Chamber of Commerce. "Visitor Information." http://www.frederickokchamber.org/ (accessed October 7, 2013).

Frederick Enterprise. "Arrived in Frederick Last Saturday." http://www.frederickok.org/History/Roosevelt041405.htm (accessed October 7, 2013).

General Tommy Franks Leadership Institute and Museum. "Biography." http://www.tommyfranksmuseum.org/bio.html (accessed November 24, 2013).

Gire, Amanda. "Ritz Dedicated as Centennial Project Today." *Shawnee News Star*, May 30, 2008. http://www.news-star.com/article/20080530/NEWS/305309962/0/SEARCH (accessed October 24, 2013).

———. "Some Might Appreciate Such Company Loyalty." *Shawnee News Star*, November 19, 2008. http://www.news-star.com/article/20081119/NEWS/311199895/0/SEARCH (accessed October 24, 2013).

Goldsmith, Earl. "Wetumka Makes Lemonade from Lemons." *Henryettan.* http://thehenryettan.com/index.php?option=com_content&view=article&id=1583:wetumka-makes-lemonaide-from-lemons&catid=16:opinionscolumns&Itemid=10 (accessed October 4, 2013).

Horn, Tommie L. "Marietta." Encyclopedia of Oklahoma History and Culture. http://digital.library.okstate.edu/encyclopedia/entries/M/MA024.html (accessed October 23, 2013).

Hotel Cherokee. National Register of Historic Places nomination form. http://www.ocgi.okstate.edu/shpo/nhrpdfs/98000200.pdf (accessed December 5, 2013).

Jackson, Ron. "In Remembrance: The Hammon Flood of April 1934 Survivor Shoulders the Memories." *Oklahoman*, April 3,2004. http://newsok.com/in-remembrance-the-hammon-flood-of-april-1934brsurvivor-shoulders-the-memories/article/1896842/?page=1 (accessed October 15, 2013).

"James Bigheart." Pamphlet from Bigheart Museum, October 5, 2013.

James W. Green v. Haskell County Board of Commissioners, et al. United States Court of Appeals for the Tenth Circuit. June 8, 2009. http://morelaw.com/verdicts/case.asp?d=40338&n=06-7098&s=OK (accessed December 1, 2013).

Krebs Heritage Museum. Pamphlet. December 10, 2013.

Lane Cabin. National Register of Historic Places nomination form. http://www.ocgi.okstate.edu/shpo/nhrpdfs/74001654.pdf (accessed December 26, 2013).

Lucille's OK. "History." http://lucillesok.com/history/ (accessed October 3, 2013).

Main Street Duncan. http://www.mainstreetduncan.net/index.html (accessed October 19, 2013).

Manske, Stan. "The Bombing of Boise City." Fiftieth anniversary memorial dedication speech. Boise City, Oklahoma, July 5,1993.

May, John D. "Barnsdall." Encyclopedia of Oklahoma History and Culture. http://digital.library.okstate.edu/encyclopedia/entries/b/ba023.html (accessed October 10, 2013).

———. "Ochelata." Encyclopedia of Oklahoma History and Culture. http://digital.library.okstate.edu/encyclopedia/entries/O/OC001.html (accessed November 6, 2013).

———. "Osage Murders." Encyclopedia of Oklahoma History and Culture, http://digital.library.okstate.edu/encyclopedia/entries/O/OS005.html (accessed October 10, 2013)

McSwain Theatre. "The History of the McSwain." http://www.mcswaintheatre.com/index_186.htm (accessed October 6, 2013).

"Memories Linger in Oilman's Restored Home." *Oklahoman*, August 25, 1985. http://newsok.com/memories-linger-in-oilmans-restored-home/article/2118980 (accessed October 17, 2013).

Miami Convention and Visitors Bureau. *Miami Official Visitors Guide*. October 31, 2013.

"Mickey Mantle, Bio—Life of a Legend." Mickey Mantle website. http://www.mickeymantle.com/bio.htm (accessed November 10, 2013).

"Miranda Loads the Pink Pistol for Grand Opening." Miranda Lambert website. http://www.mirandalambert.com/news/article.php?article=355 (accessed January 18, 2014).

Oklahoma Territorial Plaza. http://www.okterritory.org/ (accessed October 4, 2013).

Otoe-Missouria Tribe. "History." http://www.omtribe.org/index.php?culture-history (accessed October 3, 2013).

Pete's Place. "History." http://www.petes.org/history.html (accessed December 11, 2013).

Ralston Opera House. National Register of Historic Places inventory nomination form. http://www.ocgi.okstate.edu/shpo/nhrpdfs/87001257.pdf (accessed October 9, 2013).

Sandstone Creek Watershed Project. Oklahoma Conservation Commission, October 2011. http://www.ok.gov/conservation/documents/Sandstone%20Creek%20Watershed%20-%20Roger%20Mills%20Co..pdf (accessed October 15, 2013).

Seminole Producer. "The History of the Seminole Producer." http://www.seminoleproducer.com/producerhistory.htm (accessed October 21, 2013).

Stotts, Melinda. "The Store Burns Up in Bluejacket." *Miami News-Record*, July 5, 2012. http://www.miamiok.com/news/article_0914660a-c6c3-11e1-bc68-001a4bcf887a.html (accessed November 7, 2013).

"Supreme Court Lets Ruling Stand That Religious Monument at Oklahoma Courthouse Is Unconstitutional." American Civil Liberties Union, March 10, 2010. https://www.aclu.org/religion-belief/supreme-court-lets

-ruling-stand-religious-monument-oklahoma-courthouse-unconstitutio (accessed December 1, 2013).

Tillman Historical Society. "The Remarkable Abernathys." http://tillmanokhistory.org/RemarkableAbernathys.htm (accessed October 7, 2013).

Timberlake Rose Rock Museum. "History." http://www.roserockmuseum.com/history.html (accessed October 3, 2013).

Times Record. "LeFlore Commission Approves Ten Commandments Monument for Courthouse Lawn." April 7, 2013. http://swtimes.com/sections/news/leflore-commission-approves-ten-commandments-monument-courthouse-lawn.html (accessed December 1, 2013).

Top of Oklahoma Museum. Pamphlet. August 31, 2013.

Tramel, Berry. "Binger Residents Announce Plans to Build Bench Museum." *Oklahoman*, May 9, 2008. http://newsok.com/binger-residents-announce-plans-to-build-bench-museumbrspan-classhl2hall-of-famer-will-be-in-oklahoma-city-on-may-18span/article/3241060/?page=1 (accessed October 25, 2013).

Tuton's Drugstore. National Register of Historic Places nomination form. http://www.ocgi.okstate.edu/shpo/nhrpdfs/80003278.pdf (accessed February 2, 2014).

Wagoner Chamber of Commerce. "History." http://www.thecityofwagoner.org/history.php (accessed November 23, 2013).

"Wayne Holden." *Oklahoman*, March 1, 2009. http://www.legacy.com/obituaries/oklahoman/obituary.aspx?pid=124722081 (accessed October 19, 2013).

Wilson, Linda D. "Ralston." Encyclopedia of Oklahoma History and Culture. http://digital.library.okstate.edu/encyclopedia/entries/R/RA007.html (accessed October 9, 2013).

Wilson, Raymond. "Geronimo." Encyclopedia of Oklahoma History and Culture. http://digital.library.okstate.edu/encyclopedia/entries/G/GE009.html (accessed October 3, 2013).

Woodward, Sommer. "Honoring a Legend." *Pryor Times*, October 23, 2006. http://pryordailytimes.com/local/x519308065/Honoring-a-legend/print (accessed November 10, 2013).

Woodward Theatre. National Register of Historic Places registration form. http://www.ocgi.okstate.edu/shpo/nhrpdfs/08001153.pdf (accessed January 5, 2014).

"World Championship Cow Chip Throwing Contest." Beaver Chamber of Commerce. http://www.beavercountychamberofcommerce.com/page11.html (accessed December 26, 2013).

Wright, Chris. "Ochelata Building Set on Fire." KOTV News on 6, January 21, 2009. http://www.newson6.com/story/9710786/ochelata-building-set-on-fire (accessed November 6, 2013).

About the Author

Kristi Eaton is a journalist based in Oklahoma City. A native of Tulsa, she lived in Arizona, Italy, Saipan and South Dakota before returning to Oklahoma. She holds a bachelor of arts in journalism from Arizona State University. Her stories have been published in the *Washington Post*, *Miami Herald*, *San Francisco Chronicle* and elsewhere.